PRAISE FOR MY HAPPY PLACE

"Success is so much more than a paycheck. For each of us to be truly happy, our work and lives need to strike a better balance. Katie's powerful story proves the mainstream American concept of living the dream isn't necessarily everyone's ideal."

— ALEJANDRO BEDOYA, PROFESSIONAL SOCCER PLAYER, PHILADELPHIA UNION CAPTAIN, U.S. MEN'S NATIONAL TEAM

"Katie's writing is so authentic, you don't even feel like you're reading. You feel like you're part of a great conversation. Be ready to cry a little and laugh a LOT. *My Happy Place* is both painful and uplifting, and filled with practical advice to find your own joy."

— CHRIS JANSEN, HEAD OF U.S. NEWS AND PUBLISHING, GOOGLE

"Katie's book is inspiring, relatable, humorous and a breath of fresh air! This is a wonderful book that will motivate you as well!"

— Dr. Jennifer Caudle, Family Physician, TV Health Expert, Associate Professor, Rowan University

MY HAPPY PLACE

MY HAPPY PLACE

HOW I DIY'D MY OWN BLISS

KATIE FEHLINGER

Copyright © 2020 by Katie Fehlinger

All rights reserved.

No part of this book may be reproduced in any form or by any electronic or mechanical means, including information storage and retrieval systems, without written permission from the author, except for the use of brief quotations in a book review and certain other noncommercial uses permitted by copyright law.

The anecdotes in this book are based on true events and the author's recollection, but some names and identifying details have been changed for privacy reasons.

Katie Fehlinger's website: www.katiefehlinger.com

ISBN 978-1-7351479-0-1: Paperback

ISBN 978-1-7351479-1-8: Ebook

Editor: Nicole Rollender

Cover design: Josh Gragg

First Edition

CONTENTS

Prologue	1

PART I

1. Realizing What Doesn't Make You Happy	9
2. Focusing on What Matters	33
3. The Mental Shift	57
4. The Active Shift	81

PART II

5. Rise Above Everyone's Pressure	103
6. Expect Nothing	125
7. Embrace the Cliche	139
8. Beat the Crap Out of Internal Battles	161

PART III

9. Fearlessly Be Yourself	181
10. Fearlessly Better Yourself	195
11. Have A Good Show	217
Acknowledgments	243
My Top 10 Resources	247

PROLOGUE

The day I hit absolute bottom, I had the afternoon to myself.

My then 2-year-old twin daughters were sleeping over at their grandparents' house, while my husband traveled for work. On days like this, I took advantage of the quiet. I'd drift into a well-deserved mid-afternoon nap. I'd binge-watch a few episodes of "Girlfriends' Guide to Divorce." I'd pop a frozen pizza into the oven and wait until the pan cooled enough so I could eat the whole damn pie straight from it. (One less dish to wash, after all.)

But on this day, comfort eating and TiVo were the farthest things from my mind. I pulled into the garage after a harrowing day at work, my large sunglasses hiding fresh tears and splotchy cheeks. For the bulk of my half-hour commute home, I had sobbed.

My body and mind felt heavy, achy and worn out. I trudged into the silent, still house, my feet weighted like bricks. With a sigh of exhaustion, I let my bag drop on the hall table. I dragged myself upstairs to twist my hair into a top knot and replace my sweaty ballet flats, Spanx and dress (that was getting way too tight) with oversized sweats and a T-shirt.

I came back downstairs. Next thing I knew, I had huddled myself in the fetal position under my kitchen island, ugly crying loudly and uncontrollably.

Eventually, I shrieked, "WHAT'S WRONG WITH MEEEEEEEE?!?!?!"

The hardwood floors echoed back my voice as I lay alone in my empty house. In that hollow sound, I witnessed the vastness of my fatigue and desperation.

Let me tell you about my ugly cry. It's akin to the guy in the "Leave Britney Alone" YouTube video in its fervor, but over the top in every way.

This isn't something I do often. I've ugly cried at the "Christian the Lion" YouTube video—you know, the heartstring-pulling one where two guys raise a lion cub, release him to the wild when he gets too big, and then reunite with him years later in Africa, Whitney Houston's tear-inducing song "I Will Always Love You" playing all the while.

Prologue

I ugly cried at the movie "Marley & Me," when the family had to put their beloved dog to sleep.

I'm pretty sure my joyous sobbing when two of my dearest friends got engaged at a Penn State tailgate probably goes under the ugly cry column, too.

But this ugly cry wasn't like any other. None of my tearful episodes ever sprung from a place as distraught as this. In that moment, total despair had overtaken me.

NOTHING SEEMED RIGHT. I worried that I wasn't showing up for my little girls. I told myself that I was an uncaring spouse. I despised my job. I was lost in a prison of my own design, in a slump that buried me.

I was simply and uncategorically unhappy.

I stayed in that slump for months, functioning in a near-constant state of irritation, especially at work. I snapped at everyone, including my husband and daughters. Finally, I couldn't stand it any longer.

I had to make a life-altering choice.

"It's time to take care of your shit, girl," I told myself. "Either you put up with your situation, or fix it."

I needed saving.

I also knew damn well no one would do it for me but *myself*.

. . .

THIS IS the story of how I finally discovered what truly makes me happy—and how I overcame roadblocks along the way to DIY my own personal bliss. My journey wasn't easy, but I learned that if you want to reinvent your life badly enough, you can do it. Even more importantly, I've worked hard to ensure I never fall into a similar low ever again—and I share my hard-won "hows" with you.

I hope to make you laugh out loud with some outlandish stories.

You may even tear up when you recognize your struggle in mine.

Throughout the following chapters, you'll find ninja nuggets of wisdom and motivation, along with practical hacks, advice and tips that helped me navigate the hardest choice I've ever made in my life.

I finished writing this book as an unrelenting, deadly virus swept the world and forced the closure of our communities. We all had to grapple with a new reality of social distancing, get used to new protocol of how and when we could gather with our families and friends, and deal with the mental and physical stress of our lives being upended almost entirely. So many people had to suffer unimaginable loss and life-altering struggle.

What transpired once COVID-19 hit us all made me contemplate a lot. Had I made the right decision?

Would I do things differently? Despite a new bizarre, sometimes scary reality, am I truly living each day in the moment and able to appreciate and find joy wherever I can?

The answer was a resounding YES.

I believe you can find your own authentically happy place, no matter the circumstance.

So let's get it!

PART I

RESET YOUR MINDSET

1
REALIZING WHAT DOESN'T MAKE YOU HAPPY

> " Don't you just wanna be happy?"
>
> — Gary Vaynerchuk

> " Happiness is a choice."
>
> — Ralph Marston

I t was a beautiful, mild afternoon in May 2018—and I was utterly miserable.

Cinco de Mayo and the Kentucky Derby coincided that year, and a friend had invited our family over for tacos, margaritas, mint juleps and revelry around two exciting minutes of horse racing.

Mere hours before we were expected, I texted our host, "Hey, sorry to bail last minute, but we're having a day from hell. Sorry to say, we won't be any fun. Really hope we can get a raincheck! Preakness or Belmont?"

Now.

Here's what I was *actually* trying to say in that text: "Hey, sorry to bail last minute, but if I try to socialize today, I'll lash out at someone unintentionally and compound the guilt I already feel (as well as suffer extreme embarrassment after the fact). I'm fairly certain I have something close to clinical depression. I'm sad, tearful, angry and irritable all at once. I can't turn it off. I don't even know why I'm upset. I'm exhausted and restless at the same time. Also, I've been hiding out from my family in my dark bedroom on this gorgeous Cinco de Mayo Saturday. That's making me feel even more pathetic and sorry for myself. I'm in an emotional spiral and don't know whether I'll recover. But have a margarita for me!"

Anyone else hear the invisible record screech to dead silence? More importantly, how did I get here?

Well, folks, it was a classic woke-up-on-the-wrong-side-of-the-bed morning. Of course, I hadn't had enough sleep. That was nothing new, though. As I came downstairs to get breakfast for my toddler twins, I knew

I was in for a rough day. (And I was already dreading the visit to my friend's place later.)

This wasn't the commonplace exhausted-parent story. You know, where weeks in advance, in the late morning when you're still bright-eyed and bushy-tailed, you excitedly make plans to meet up with friends: "Oh my gosh, it'll be so fun! We'll start with happy hour, continue on to dinner and then after-party with more drinks at a bar with live music!" Then the actual day rolls around, and you're so pooped that all you want to do is go to bed at 9 p.m.

Oh no, this was far different. I was enmeshed in a negative mindset. Uncontrolled aggravation. I wanted nothing to do with anyone from the second I woke up. I wish I could have gone back to bed and tried a reset that morning. But my girls were asking for breakfast and my husband was still asleep, so it was my turn.

After angrily toasting two blueberry waffles for them, I slammed my butter knife down and went out on the deck for peace and quiet. Surely the bird song, the sweet grassy smell and a big ole brew from the Keurig (dark roast, two packets of Truvia and a large splash of hazelnut Coffee mate creamer) would perk me up.

My husband Steve, who had sleepily made his way down to the kitchen, knew something was wrong. He awkwardly made side glances at me, trying to figure out where my mood was coming from. When I had days like this, he usually kept his distance, didn't say much to me, and I preferred it that way. But this time, he tried to gently help me feel better. He opened the door onto the deck so our blond-haired little ones could rush out to see me. Besides my cats, no one has ever shown me such unconditional love. These tiny people put up with me at my most scatterbrained, exasperated and frustrated. They just loved me, no matter what. As they toddled over to give me a snuggle, my tears welled at the half-hearted embrace I mustered up in return.

My internal sadness turned to disgust at what I did next.

I got up and left. I actually walked away from my girls as they tried to wrap their arms around me and lean their heads against me. All I could mentally stand to do was get up, pull away from them and walk away. Because I was so messed up on the inside that morning, I couldn't handle being with them—or anyone. Instead, I holed up in my bedroom with my tumultuous feelings and a library book, praying it would all pass.

It never did. The whole morning ticked away and I felt even worse. As the hour hand passed noon, my dread mounted. How could I possibly socialize with my friends when I felt this way? I couldn't even summon the energy to change from my worn-out Cedar Crest College sweatpants and tattered oversized pub crawl T-shirt.

And so I sent that vague text: "Hey, sorry to bail last minute..." Thankfully, my friend wrote a non-judgmental message back expressing kind regrets that we wouldn't make it.

Two days later, I wrote her back to say thanks: "I'm so sorry we couldn't make it. We've got stuff going on, and there's a lot to unpack there. Really hope we can reschedule, but thanks for understanding."

Wow. I had single-handedly ruined what should have been a fun afternoon with friends. Even worse, through those texts, I passed the burden onto my family. This wasn't *our* problem. No. It was my problem. I felt even more shame.

Unfortunately, Cinco de Mayo didn't stand alone. 2018 was a hell of a year for me.

THERE'S NO MAGIC PILL

My short-term memory may be a joke, but I know exactly how every day played out that year because I documented my emotional and psychological state every day.

Whaaaaaaaat?

OK, let me explain. I had bought a day planner to stay organized and ahead. But this cute little spiral-bound notebook was more than just to-do lists, appointments and budget planning. It was a close duplicate to a bullet journal. There was a section of perforated shopping lists to fill out and take to the grocery store. The notebook came with cute stickers to highlight events on the calendar pages: a cartoon life preserver with the caption "Vacation," an airplane for "Travel" days, a confetti popper to indicate when it was time to "Party," and stickers for all of the holidays. My inner arts-and-craft geek had a field day placing those stickers throughout 2018, what I hoped would be a banner year of perfect planning.

Although I transferred most of my schedule to Google Calendar in 2018, that spiral-bound planner served me long after the year ended. It included an interesting feature called the Year in Pixels: 365 little boxes representing each day. The idea? Shade each box with a color representing how you felt or the kind of day you had.

So why not? I did it. Each evening in 2018, I evaluated my mood during the day. Had I felt "Terrific" (hot pink)? "Good" (orange)? "Just OK" (green)? "Sad" (gray)? Or "Miserable" (black)? Believe me, I diligently filled out this chart. When January 1, 2019 dawned, I reviewed my mood over the course of an entire year, all laid out like a mosaic.

Admittedly, I remember giving my daily temperament the benefit of the doubt. A lot of my "OK" days were me trying to trick myself into believing I was happier than I was. No joke, even on my "Just OK" days, I could have been an extra for "My So-Called Life." I moped, I huffed, and I went through the motions. I literally put my head on my desk at work when no one was looking and tried—often unsuccessfully—to smile through my distress.

So let's see: I had generally "OK" days (to be taken with a grain of salt) and a handful of "Good" days. That left lots of orange and green boxes speckled on my year's grid. There weren't enough "Terrific" days—only a handful of shaded hot pink boxes. (Those almost exclusively fell on days I wasn't in the office.) There were lots of gray "Sad" days. My Year in Pixels was a fascinating, eye-opening overview of my life, all summed up on a single page. Of course, we all have bad days, but this was simply too many.

I only shaded two days in "Miserable" black. One was the day I ugly cried alone under the kitchen island. The other—Cinco de Mayo. I couldn't get those days back. Something had to give, since something was clearly very wrong. And there it all was in Crayola marker technicolor in my day planner: documented proof of my less-than-ideal circumstances over the course of an entire year.

There had to be a medical explanation for this, right? Following that horrible 24 hours on May 5, 2018, I spent the next several days wearing out Google search:

How late can postpartum depression set in? What are the signs of clinical depression? How do menstrual hormones change after childbirth? Do I just need a crap-ton of therapy?

I researched my problem into oblivion. When I finally let my search engine come up for air, I convinced myself that I had Premenstrual Dysphoric Disorder, or PMDD, essentially PMS on steroids. Seven to 10 days before your period, you experience a range of really-over-the-top emotions. This had to be my problem, right? The timing worked out. I had a year's worth of documented calendar proof and a menstrual cycle that ran like clockwork. And without fail, somewhere within the 10 days leading up to my period, those gray and black days showed up on my homemade motley matrix.

I worked through exploring PMDD with my doctor. I presented her with my year-long record of evidence. I explained my symptoms. Together, we agreed that I should medicate the problem. She gave me anti-depressant medication to keep on standby, to be taken on an as-needed basis (once or twice a month in my case).

I have to confess, I was reluctant taking these pills. I followed my doctor's instructions and only took my medication when I really needed it. But right or wrong—and despite my legitimate need for them—I couldn't shake the belief that the little tablets I loathsomely called my "happy pills" were a cop out. I had a nagging feeling, as though I'd given in to medicating myself, as if this prescription was the only method available for me to achieve a mood lift.

I was also terrified that I'd develop an addiction, and I wasn't willing to let that happen. Thankfully, it didn't. In fact, looking back honestly, I probably should've taken a pill on a handful of other days.

Still, the pills gave me enough of a mood boost to power through bouts of overwhelming stress, irritation and anger. But as I took them over the course of several months, I realized they weren't enough. I needed total contentment. And despite the hit of temporary uplift those pills sparked in me, I simply couldn't achieve that on meds alone. Deep down, I understood that. A hit from my little orange prescription bottle may have helped me work through the worst of my moodiest days, but it wasn't a magic pill.

TIME FOR A MASSIVE LIFE SHIFT

Here was my deal: If I wanted to find lasting joy in the purest sense, I needed to make a big life change. Yet at the time, I couldn't grasp this. That simple truth was stuffed and hidden away so well in my subconscious that I just didn't recognize it.

And so, rather than think how—let alone even

begin—to take action to change my circumstances, I did what I always did when I felt stuck. I put up with my situation. I pushed my frustrations, anguish and all-consuming stress deep down. I spent another six months wallowing in my own resentment, taking another prescribed pill when I woke up on the wrong side of the bed.

Quite simply however, to be happy, I needed to do what makes me happy. It's so obvious. I mean, this is the in-your-face basis of this book and your expected jumping-off point. Through many months of self-evaluation, four words kept creeping into my brain like animated thought bubbles: What makes you happy? What brings you bliss? What completely fulfills you? For a long time, I didn't know how to answer these questions.

Lots of people thought I had it made. I spent the last 15 years in the TV news business, the bulk of that time as an on-air meteorologist for a news station in Philadelphia. I met viewers at events or when they came in for station tours. They'd say, "Your job must be so much fun!" I'd always put on an enthusiastic face, my eyes wide (my smile even wider) replying, "Yes! I love it! You're right, it's so much fun!" I felt a duty to tell these people what I assumed they wanted to hear. And that fed into this: I tend toward a "make-the-best-of-it" attitude, which meant I managed to find reasons to stay in my position.

Making the best of it is great sometimes—like when you're stuck in the excruciatingly long line at Disney's Animal Kingdom waiting to ride Expedition Everest. You're waiting, after all, for the thrill of a big roller-coaster drop and state-of-the-art creature effects on your quest to see the Yeti. Knowing what awaits makes the hours of weaving through the entrance ropes worth it, and bonus, you have expertly crafted Himalayan-themed displays to peruse along the way. Or when midday summer construction on the Schuylkill Expressway takes out two of the three lanes, bringing the already-clogged traffic flow to a near standstill, you're bebopping to Hall and Oates' "I Can't Go For That" with the windows down while inching your car toward the Montgomery Drive exit. A traffic jam session can make those otherwise mind-numbing minutes a lot easier to handle.

I've pep-talked myself ad nauseum into the idea that my backwards TV schedule of waking up at 2:45 a.m. every weekday was actually good for my family: "No really, it's great! My daughters are still practically babies so I can be home by 1 p.m. to spend time with them! Since my husband works primarily from home, I get to see him, too!" The reality? I was always cranky and drained by 1:30 p.m., so I spent that free time napping or just in a daze with zero energy to even read a story to my girls. And forget living a healthy, balanced lifestyle.

But on top of that delusion, and over so many years of trying to make peace with my unsettled mind, there was always a bigger distraction to help me stay positive. Planning my wedding followed by the euphoria of having gotten married held me over for a while. Building and buying, and then furnishing our first house took up my time for a few years. Having twins really kept me occupied—and they still do. But eventually, the spray from the major-milestones hose dwindled to a trickle, and I realized I needed to tune into what I really wanted. Why was that so hard?

WHAT MAKES ME HAPPY?

At the root of this predicament? That broad initial question: What makes me happy?

Funny. I knew why I WASN'T happy.

The awful middle-of-the-night alarm was getting old.

I had no motivation. Like zero. For almost anything.

My morale was so freaking low. Whether it was warranted or not, I felt utterly unappreciated and invisible in my job.

I ran on a hamster wheel on autopilot, but never actually got anywhere different.

Look, I don't take for granted for one second that the career path I landed on is desirable. I was incredibly lucky for so many reasons. I started out with a salary nearly double what most college grads snagged their first year out of journalism or broadcasting school—a whopping $30,000. I got to stay in the Northeast, within a three-hour drive of my family for my entire career. I received opportunities that, trust me, I know a lot of people don't get.

The strange delight of Zach Galifianakis creepily photobombing my weather hit.

The totally normal delight of Tony Danza serenading me with a ukulele.

The sheer glee at getting to introduce Gritty, the Philadelphia Flyers' new mascot, to the city in his TV debut. (Did you know his belly button squeaks?)

The invaluable professional experience of delivering national weather reports for ABC, ESPN, CBS, Fox News, Bloomberg, Big Ten Network, Fox Sports Network and others, all from a cozy college town studio.

I also knew what I didn't want to do.

I didn't want to continue feeling like my soul was being sucked out of me. (No one ever accused me of under-exaggerating.)

I didn't want to be a slave to a rigorous schedule that put a constant glaze over my eyes, left me worn out and grouchy, with virtually no social life. It's not a stretch to say that I spent the bulk of my 30s in a weary haze.

Most heart-wrenching for me, I didn't want to miss out on my girls growing up. I didn't want to be totally beat every single time they asked me to color with them or to sample the concoction they created for me in their play kitchen. I came home so spent that I couldn't drag myself to the toy chest to pull down Candyland from the high shelf when they asked me to play with them. This devastated me.

And then, missing their milestones, due to an antiquated system of TV "sweeps." These are the three months out of the year when most news people can't take time off: February, May and November. That meant I had to miss my daughters' end-of-year preschool party. The day of their special shindig, I sat in my drab windowless office, glued to my iPhone. Ten miles away, I watched on FaceTime as my girls played in the sandbox, took a nature hike to the bird lookout and stood in line for pizza. I was so bummed that I missed out.

I really wasn't OK with staying in a "dream career" that forced me to miss a lifetime of special moments.

I needed to stop lying to myself.

I needed to do what brought ME joy.

I knew I had what others would kill for and felt insanely guilty that I didn't want it. Granted, I was really good at being an on-air meteorologist and I put in the hard work to get there. However, I tried to convince myself that my path was the stuff my true dreams were made of—when it was actually just misguided gratitude for someone else's dream life.

Remember: Just because others might want your situation doesn't mean it's YOUR ideal. One woman's trash is most definitely another woman's treasure. (I should know: As a DIY gal, I've pulled a dusty, grime-covered window frame out of a barn loft to make decorative wall art that would make Joanna Gaines proud.) While I enjoyed a successful career, my job success ranked nowhere close to the top of my "Things I Treasure Most" list.

Bottom line: My career path and its resulting lifestyle wasn't my most honest path to happiness. Ziggy Marley once said, "You can complain because roses have thorns or you can rejoice because thorns have roses." I genuinely attempted to view the glass as half full. I tried to focus on the positives of an overnight schedule, the time with Steve that I knew fellow colleagues couldn't snag with their significant others, the joy of knowing I'd have every afternoon with the girls, and weekends off—hallelujah! (I mean, talk about a blessing in the news business.)

Oddly, trying to turn my focus to all these reasons why I should be happy with the status quo actually made me feel worse. I'd say to myself, "I have so many blessings in my life. Damn girl, aren't you ashamed that this isn't enough to give you joy?"

Tumultuous though it was, 2018 turned out to be my year of massive realization.

ELLE WOODS IS MY GIRL

Have you ever heard a song or watched a movie that spoke right to you? It's happened to me a few times.

In high school, Alanis Morissette's "Jagged Little Pill" album spoke to my soul. Her song, "You Oughta Know," became my anthem following a bad breakup. That guy was my first. First love, first angst, first full-blown relationship, first everything. And he dumped my rebellious and emotionally fragile ass in a note he passed to me between classes on a Friday. By Monday, he was dating a new, Pollyanna-by-comparison girl. (He later married her and they had a few kids.) Man, that breakup jerked my heart in so many directions.

Then in my early 20s, the fabulous Elle Woods came along. The "Legally Blonde" plotline stood for my struggle like my own personal Statue of Liberty, lifting her lamp beside the golden blonde door. When Elle got into Harvard Law School, I found my spirit sister in this young female character who pursued her dreams, despite the haters and naysayers. Even though she chased a law degree initially for all the wrong reasons, she figured it out in the end. The outcome is what's important, right?

Remember when poor Elle gets tricked into dressing up like a sexy pink bunny for a house party that wasn't actually a costumed get-together? My heart always hurts for Elle in this scene. Not only does she get tricked by two insecure mean girls, but she gets lambasted by her lame ex-boyfriend, Warner. He thinks he's opening Elle's eyes, helping her understand that she's simply not intelligent enough to succeed at something as difficult as law school.

I'd been in Elle's shoes. Several times. In middle school algebra class, I couldn't grasp the concept of absolute value. When I asked my teacher to explain it again, she accused me of not paying attention and actually mocked me. I felt like an idiot in front of my whole class.

In high school chemistry, the teacher called on me to recite a formula we'd learned the day before. I never raised my hand purposely in class, because this teacher was one of those senior tenured types. He was so jaded by decades of dealing with punk teenagers that he thrived on making his students feel inadequate. My cheeks flushed deep pink as I meekly told him I didn't know the answer, but he wouldn't accept that. Instead, he pushed me to answer the question by giving me unhelpful hints and patronizing me in front of a judgmental room of my fellow classmates, many of whom seemed to enjoy his mockery of my intelligence.

The disrespect got more demeaning. There was the guy I dated who actually admitted he was embarrassed to introduce me to his family. In his words, I wasn't "the type you bring home to Mom". Later a different guy, after we'd had a heated argument over what started as an educated debate, told me he liked me better when our relationship was just about the physical. He had no need for my mental contribution.

Ouch, boys. Those put-downs seared into my brain.

So yes, Elle Woods' determination to overcome the bullshit in her life still holds a very special place in my heart. Moreover, I channel a particular sequence in that movie as motivation. As bunny-costumed Elle storms out of the non-costumed party declaring, "I'll show you how valuable Elle Woods can be," the catchy bass line of Joanna Pacitti's "Watch Me Shine" begins an underscore.

This leads into a montage of Elle busting her ass to do the work: She waits in line to purchase her new laptop. She writes the shit out of a term paper. Cut to Elle, as she purposefully walks past her enemies with a stack of books she'll study in the library. Next, she impresses her professor by answering a question that demonstrates she clearly read and understood the material. And she multitasks like a mofo, reading a thick textbook and watching court TV, all while getting in her cardio on the elliptical. Girlfriend still keeps up appearances too, as she takes notes on civil procedure while under the salon dryer.

This sequence of Elle working diligently, coupled with the rousing "Watch Me Shine" spoke to me at that time. I blasted that song as I drove to classes. I blasted it in my Discman as I studied. I blasted that song as I worked out, too. And it helped get me past the image of myself that a few jerk boyfriends and supposed friends projected onto me.

I'M TRAPPED IN A CHRISTMAS MOVIE

Many years later, another movie character spoke to the depths of my being. This silver-screen performance caught me metaphorically in a deep coma-esque sleep and trumpeted an air horn next to my ear lobe. The person holding the air horn was Dermot Mulroney.

Dermot Mulroney? "Wait," you may be thinking. "That's the guy from 'My Best Friend's Wedding.'" Yes. Yes, he is.

Allow me to explain.

I'm one of those people who can't get enough of the winter holidays. I start listening to Christmas music in November, typically around Election Day. (That's probably not a coincidence. OK, it's definitely not a coincidence.)

It gives me joy to build traditions with my family, hear the sounds of the season and watch a ton of Christmas movies. I have an old DVD spindle (coined my "Spindle of Joy") that's stacked with 30 Christmas movies. I try to watch all of them at least once over the span of the season leading up to the holiday.

What I love so much about Christmas movies is there's one for every mood. If I'm feeling sentimental, I pop in "It's a Wonderful Life." If I'm feeling traditional, I play "A Christmas Carol," "Miracle on 34th Street" or "Meet Me in St. Louis." If it's nostalgia I'm after, I choose "White Christmas." If I want to laugh out loud, it's "Elf." No question.

If I'm feeling emotional and want a heart tugger, I pull out "The Family Stone." Oh, how I adore this movie. Steve meanwhile, hates it. I made him watch it with me once, and he cringed through the whole thing because Sarah Jessica Parker's character reminded him of an ex. I get it. From the stories I heard, she was pretty uptight.

 Now I watch the movie solo every holiday season, and I've grown to prefer it that way. The last four years, I've made it a habit to wake up before everyone else on a weekend morning in early December and sneak down to the basement to watch this flick alone. By the way, this movie boasts an A-list cast: Diane Keaton, Craig T. Nelson, Rachel McAdams, Claire Danes, Luke Wilson and Sarah Jessica Parker. Dermot Mulroney plays Everett, the character I relate to the most.

Everett, a polished businessman, has achieved almost "everything." He's living the corporate life in New York, with an accomplished girlfriend by his side. He believes the next step on his successful path is to put a ring on her finger. The main plot takes place as Everett brings his girlfriend home to meet his family for the first time at the holidays, with a plan to propose to her. However, his family (and the audience) realize that she is totally wrong for him.

This holiday homecoming pushes Everett to the realization that his current life path won't ultimately make him happy. "Do you feel like you chose your life?" Everett asks Claire Danes' character Julie, who had a job and life she loved. "Said, 'This is the thing I'm gonna do. These are the things I want.' Not necessarily because you were good at this thing or because everybody told you that that's what you should want, because everybody said that's who you were?"

The lessons and themes in this movie are freakishly parallel to what I was experiencing. I never actually realized that until I'd seen the movie several dozen times.

Man, hindsight is 20/20.

It's so clear to me now that I was staring in a mirror on repeat every holiday season, with the very same internal conflict Dermot Mulroney's character faced.

I watched my beloved movie during the 2018 Christmas season one Saturday morning at 5:45 a.m, as I wrapped presents before anyone woke up. But as the symbolic scenes played out, my nimble hands slowed way down. Eventually, I just stopped multitasking and curled up on the couch with my coffee to give the plot full attention.

This movie always makes me cry. The story is a tearjerker anyway, but my tears welled that morning for another reason: because it had finally, truly hit me.

My happiness isn't defined by anyone else. What you're *supposed* to want isn't necessarily the key to living your personal joy.

Take city living. A lot of my colleagues and friends live in Philadelphia or New York. They love it. Everything's available: You can get takeout in any cuisine within a two-mile radius. The commute is simpler without a car. You can walk, bike, train or Uber everywhere.

But I absolutely hate city living. It's just not something I'd choose.

You see, I'm much more of a backyard type. Give me suburban sprawl, three times the house for what you'd pay in the city and the smell of freshly cut grass. I love pulling my car into the grocery store parking lot and loading up my trunk myself. That's actual, pure delight for me right there.

OK, so I know without a shadow of a doubt that I prefer suburbs to a city. I also know without even thinking that:

- "Sleeping Beauty" is my all-time favorite Disney movie.
- Hazelnut coffee is my number one jam when I need caffeine.
- I prefer the mountains to the beach.
- I'll shop online as opposed to a brick-and-mortar store any day.
- I'm capable of maintaining a disciplined diet, if there's no junk food in the house.
- Yoga is the only workout I'll never need motivation to complete.
- My favorite weather? Simple. A sunny day in the mid-70s, with light wind and low dew points (the ultimate perfect hair day).

However, something kept me from saying, "This is the life path I want. I'm going to make this happen for myself, no matter what anyone else says."

It's fear. Unshakeable fear. I was afraid of judgment, of ridicule, of concern from others, of the risk involved.

Hell, I was afraid of pity. These are clearly really big hurdles, but I knew better. My choice: change course or continue to suffer. The days of just trying to get through would continue indefinitely unless I did something about it, but I'm the girl who'll make every excuse in the world when the stakes are as high as this. I needed a lot of pushing from every angle. This big epiphany alone wasn't going to make me plunge into the unknown with this much uncertainty.

Nope. To shake my life up, it took something far more profound—something that hit entirely too close to home.

2
FOCUSING ON WHAT MATTERS

❝ Left foot, right foot, breathe."

— Pat Summitt

❝ We are stronger than we will ever know until we know it."

— Stephanie Bloom

It was a rare moment of quiet.
I was plopped in the middle of the couch with my feet on the coffee table, one little blonde toddler snuggled on each side of me, their attention

consumed by "Paw Patrol." I mindlessly scrolled through my Facebook feed, enjoying the tranquility, when a certain post caught my attention. I jolted upright, unsettling the girls from their cartoon.

"Oh my god," I uttered, stock still as my mind tried to process what was on the screen.

"My heart is shattered," the post began and then shared the gut-wrenching news that Kevin, a dear friend of ours, had just lost the love of his life to cancer.

My husband Steve had introduced me to Kevin and his wife Steph at a Penn State football weekend when we had just started dating. At the time, I was pretty new to the PSU football experience. Flocks of Steve's friends came into town for home games and crashed at his place. I felt timid as the new girlfriend around so many of them at once. But I totally gravitated to Steph. She was one of those people who talked comfortably to any stranger in the room, and her welcoming personality put my nerves at ease.

I had moved to the area to take a broadcasting position at AccuWeather, but ended up getting so much more than just a job out of the deal. One evening, soon after I'd moved to State College, PA, I joined a group of my new coworkers for happy hour. I hadn't had the chance to meet everyone yet, and when I arrived only one chair remained at the table next to this super cute, charming guy with salt and pepper hair and an adorable crooked smile. His name was Steve and we had a ton in common.

Fast forward a few years: Steve and I exchanged vows on a sunny Caribbean beach and Kevin and Steph were there among a small handful of close friends and family.

These two had a plan early on to build their dream life—to live in California's near-perfect climate close to the beach. They'd already made the cross-country move and gotten married in the Santa Ynez Valley.

Because it was on the West Coast, Kevin and Steph jokingly (but seriously) made an informal promise to their Penn State friends: If you come to our wedding, we'll come to yours, no matter how far away. And they totally lived up to that promise, traveling to friends' wedding venues ranging from Paris to Poland, Oyster Bay to Berlin. However, in Kevin's words, "A celebration of love for people we love, with booze and dancing? Sign us up."

Steve and I got married six years after Kevin and Steph tied their own knot. While we wouldn't change a thing about that day, we didn't make it easy on our guests. Instead, we said, "Hey, why don't you guys spend a bunch of money and vacation time and fly to Jamaica for a few days to watch us get hitched?"

By this point, Kevin and Steph had lots of life to take care of, but especially, two sweet— and very young—

boys. Were there ever an excuse to bail on an expensive trip (paradise though it was), tiny tots at home was it.

Yet sure enough, Kevin and Steph flew in to celebrate with us.

And so, for four days, I lounged on a beach with Steph and got to know her even better. We sat, fruity adult beverages in hand at 10:30 a.m., just bullshitting about anything. After a few hours in the strong Jamaican sun, we'd take a break, and then end up at the pool bar with fresh drinks and a fresh setting in which to lounge. Later in the afternoon, I'd see her FaceTiming with her little ones back home. Oh, the joy it brought her.

I was still many years away from having my own kids, so I didn't grasp how difficult it was to leave children this young for even a few days. Steph gave me mama goals. She loved those little babes so damn much. She was an epitome of a proud, loving mother. Seeing her face light up as she cooed to Benny Ben and her littlest Jack touched my heart. Now as a mother myself, I appreciate even more how sweet it really was.

Isn't it amazing the impact you can make on another person without realizing it?

It turned out that this amazing lady would impact me again, in a far more meaningful way.

Roughly five-and-a-half years after our wedding, I saw a Facebook post from Steph, featuring a video rallying all her courage as she stood at the brink of a rocky ledge: "One year ago I was reminded that the year before I jumped off a cliff at the beautiful green cave in Vis Croatia into beautiful blue water... that took everything I thought I had... I figure if I can do that, I can battle this brain tumor (which FYI is NOWHERE as beautiful as this place was)... 'right foot, left foot, breathe' #NextTuesdayIsGoingToSuckForThisTumorAtCityOfHope #StephanieIsStrongerThanThisTumor"

'RIGHT FOOT, LEFT FOOT, BREATHE'

I must have reread that post 10 times. I kept thinking I had it wrong.

Brain cancer? Not Steph. She's so young, she's got her little ones, she's got Kevin, she's got so much left to do. There's no way this is true. This is completely wrong. My mind left a trail of disbelief and shock at the vast unfairness of it all.

And then, what followed.

What came next was a battle only a true warrior could face. And Steph? Please understand me. This woman was a wonder. She fought the disease bravely. And she fought it publicly, putting out her story as a diary to the world on Facebook.

All of Steph's friends followed her on social media as she mentally prepped for the battle ahead. We watched as her son Jack named the tumor. He called it Mort, short for Voldemort. The day before she went into surgery to remove the tumor from her brain, she posted twice, only writing her battle-cry hashtag: #StephanieIsStrongerThanThisTumor. Her first pre-surgery post was a beach selfie with Ben, her oldest son, capturing a moment during their fun-filled day of surfing. The two of them beamed at the camera, having an amazing time.

The second post was a video. Steph and both of her boys lay snuggled close on the couch, looking at the camera. Two adorable little blondies, smiling sheepishly. Steph's smiling too, but not out of shyness. I recognized that smile of a mother putting on her bravest face for herself and her children. When I turned on the sound, I heard the unmistakable strength in this mama's soothing voice, coaxing her little ones to repeat after her.

"I love you," Steph says sweetly, barely audible.

"I love you," Ben and Jack say back in unison.

Steph continues, "And everything's going to be OK."

Her two boys echo with those shy smiles, "And everything is going to be OK."

Facebook kept looping this moment over and over, Steph courageously smiling through it all. "I love you. And everything is going to be OK... I love you. And everything is going to be OK." I broke down hearing her words on repeat, sobbing for Steph and her family.

Over the next year, she showed the world the raw truth of what she faced. I marveled at her courage. Within 24 hours of her brain surgery, she posted a selfie from her hospital bed, hooked up to a bunch of machines, her head totally bandaged. "I'm OK... We rocked this," she wrote. She fiercely posted pictures of what she called her "battle scars," the huge stitches sewn into the side of her half-shaved head. We got to see the superhero doctor who treated her: Her sons called him the "Fixer of Mommy's Brain." Steph took us all on her journey with her—every high and low along the way.

It's hard to comprehend how she found that kind of strength, to not only face a formidable battle this huge, but to then put herself out there for the world to see.

Damn, she was strong. But like any hero, she found her own ways to stay resilient: Seven little letters tattooed on her left arm reminded her to breathe. Later, she'd get another tattoo on her right foot with a short, powerful message addressed to herself. Using the nickname her grandpa had given her as a child—and quoting Pat Summitt, one of the most dynamite women's college basketball coaches of our time (and who'd also gone through a public battle with

Alzheimer's)—"Anniebird, remember: right foot, left foot, breathe."

The day she brushed her hair, and her shoulder-length locks started to fall out from the chemo, Steph didn't hide. She posted pictures of the brush, clumps of hair still woven in it, and a saddened selfie saying, "Warriors get to cry, too… F*~king cancer." We all journeyed with Steph through her chemo, through the days she was feeling utterly exhausted when she pronounced, "Feeling mentally stripped and broken today," with black-and-white selfies exuding pain.

She also shared fun posts about wig shopping. Steph's taste in wigs was badass: She chose a gorgeous mid-length style with blonde wavy curls, one with long bubblegum-pink locks and a mermaid look in aquamarine-to-black ombre hues. One long blue wig was fit for a superhero. Another was an epic homage to Uma Thurman in "Pulp Fiction"—a sharp, jet black bob.

Then, there was one of Steph's most vulnerable posts: It was two days before Thanksgiving, and Steph was about to go back to the doctor to get hooked up to a new medical treatment called Optune. Think of it like a 3-pound, semi-permanent skull cap to fight the return of cancer cells. She'd have to wear it 18 hours a day for a year. And she'd also need a clean-shaven head for it to be applied effectively.

And so, she holed up in the bathroom with a pair of scissors, her fierce resolve and a video camera. In the video, she doesn't say a word. It's just over two minutes of Steph, with her back to us so she can see what she's doing in the mirror. The only sound is the echo in a tiled bathroom of sharp shears slicing through chunks of hair. She looks back at the camera a few times to make sure she's still recording. Her sadness is palpable every time she looks back. But you'd never take her sadness for defeat. In her words, "Next step in this brain cancer journey... I know we're treating it so it doesn't return... and it's just hair... but this F-ING sucks."

These moments never defined her, though. Life continued. Along with her glioblastoma journey, she made other memories that we saw sprinkled in her Facebook updates: pictures of the boys' slick new haircuts and end-of-summer trips to the beach. How she rocked her long wavy pink wig at the Los Angeles Women's March, and later her green wig for school spirit day while proclaiming, "Suck it Cancer!" Then, a photo of her son Jack caught red-handed in her wigs, looking like E.T. in that part of the movie where he's disguised as a little old lady.

Videos of Ben learning to surf, pictures of the boys' first day of second and fourth grade, multiple lost-teeth offerings for the tooth fairy. Steph showed us the hip and happening walker she used to relearn how to walk, joking how she planned to gussy it up with blue-and-white streamers in honor of her beloved Penn State. Throwback pics of her and Kevin's gorgeous wedding on their anniversary (she was a stunning June bride). A simple but emphatic "We Are!!!" when Penn State beat Washington in the Fiesta Bowl, and her personalized results of the quiz, "Which Throwback Disney Movie Are You?" (Answer: "Alice in Wonderland.")

Steph still managed to uplift everyone else. After she shared an article about how Lyft was offering free rides to cancer patients, a friend commented that thanks to her, he now had a ride to and from chemo that Thursday. "Strength does not come from physical capacity. It comes from an indomitable will," she wrote, quoting Mahatma Gandhi with a collage of pics of her trip to the beach with her family that day, selfies in her sunglasses and fedora, candids with the boys, and a close-up of her bracelet emblazoned with the word "strength."

Nearly six months after her first surgery, when it was time to learn how her treatment was working, Steph shared an optimistic post: "Brain scan/MRI #2 is good!!! Doctor was happy with the scans!!! I'm sighing with relief!!!"

Nine months later, beautiful Stephanie would be gone.

'TO INFINITY AND BEYOND'

After the definitive results came back, Steph learned that the tumor had returned and she'd need to undergo yet another craniotomy. In her Facebook timeline, she posted black-and-white pictures of a tired, fierce fighter, her "breathe" tattoo dominating the foreground as she posted:

> 2 days... The countdown to brain mapping and brain surgery and drilling into hard bone and soft grey matter...begins again. I've (We've) done this before...been here before... It's just brain surgery right? Yes, it still sucks. It's still scary as hell, still terrifying, but remember to breathe... right foot, left foot, breathe... Benny, Jack, Kevin, breathe... love them forever, love carries us through... love is my biggest reason to fight."

Steph rehabbed like a champ through one last summer. The last words she posted on Facebook were a quote from Professor Dumbledore in "Harry Potter and The Prisoner of Azkaban": "Happiness can be found even in the darkest of situations if one only remembers to turn on the light."

Exactly one month later to the day of Steph's last post, Kevin was the one posting:

> My heart is shattered. Stephanie Bloom, my partner in this life, departed it this morning. She passed away at home, our first home, the only home our children have ever known. She held Ben & Jack tight on their first days in our house. They held her tight on her last days here.
>
> "My best friend is gone, but my sorrow is comforted by the knowledge of her impact on our kids. Their smarts, their wit, their kindness, their grit—are all due to her encouragement, her warmth, her love and above all by her example. I promise to continue that example, baby. And I promise to see you sometime down the road, on our next great adventure, to infinity and beyond. I love you."

At that moment, time stopped. I had a hard time grasping what had happened. Steph had fought so hard. She had been through so much. This wasn't how it was supposed to go.

Back when Steph completed the final day of her first round of chemo and radiation, she shared pictures of the mask she wore during treatment, along with a tearful video: "It's a tradition that you ring a bell three times to say 'I did it!' It was hard, it felt long and it was tiring, but I am here. I am here to celebrate life, my children, my husband, my family and my awesome army of friends...all of whom most certainly gave me the strength to get through this from seizure, to tumor, to today and to the next steps... I love you all... Thank you!!"

Steph left a hell of a legacy behind. Why wasn't I following that example?

I had no excuse.

That day was the turning point. As I processed the horrific, unfair news of what had happened to Steph and her family, a little mental flame began to burn inside me.

What was I living for? That was easy. My girls, my husband, my family, my personal contentment and joy, and an intense desire to make the most of the time I had.

How was I living for it? By getting through one day at a time. Really.

I said those words more and more, both in my head and out loud: "I'm just trying to get through. Let me just get through today. OK, only two more days until Saturday, and then I'll get a break. Ugh, just three more hours until this shift is over and I can go home."

I was literally just surviving. And that wasn't good enough anymore.

I'M WORKING FOR THE WEEKEND

Here's how a typical week broke down for me back in 2018.

It's Sunday afternoon, and a pit's started to form in my stomach knowing I'm facing another arduous week. I don't have a load of deadlines, nor does the weather forecast look particularly tricky. No, I'm merely dreading the sheer weight of my regular routine.

Begrudgingly, I prep for the week ahead. I try to make as many decisions as possible before I go to bed, to buy myself an extra minute or two of snooze time. I line up five dresses, double-checking the forecast so I'm sure my choices and sleeve length will work.

I fill up my water bottles and pack my lunch. I call it lunch, but I'm eating packaged tuna and pretzels when most people sit down to enjoy their morning coffee and breakfast. I shower, wash and dry my hair. I lay out all the beauty products and toiletries I'll need to reach for in the middle of the night rather than having to clumsily rummage through an entire drawer full of products at 2:50 a.m. Still, at least once a week, my sleep-deprived butterfingers accidentally drop something on the bathroom floor.

Personal prep out of the way, I help get the girls ready for bed. Two sets of toddler teeth to brush and floss, two sets of hands and faces to wash. If I've planned it right, we don't have to bother with baths on a Sunday.

One, usually two bedtime stories, and then snuggles and kisses goodnight before I turn on the sleep machine and the night light, and then gently close their bedroom door.

One more trip downstairs for their cups, because they realize they're thirsty and ask for water just as I shut the door. They take sips the equivalent size of a serving from a hamster-cage dropper. Then, we're on round two of "Goodnight, I love you" and forehead kisses.

One more trip downstairs to find the "Paw Patrol" action figures and library books they can't sleep without: "Make sure it's the Marshall with the black vest, not red. And it must be the Ryder with the helmet, not the scuba flippers."

"Oh, and Mama, I want the Ultimate Zuma boat. No, not that one. That's the diving vehicle."

"And I need Will and M&M." (Those are their stuffed puppies.)

"Mama, I want a flashlight. No, not that one. That's old. The butterfly flashlight."

Then, I briefly lose my shit and snap at whichever toddler is pushing my last button. I always regret it.

Finally, round three of goodnights, and I gently close the door as all little people drift off to sleep.

Now, it's lights out for me. Luckily, I can usually fall asleep on command, so if I'm beat, I just walk down the hall to my bedroom after I've won the toddler bedtime battle. But, always at the back of my mind is that nagging fact that the alarm will go off no later than 2:45 a.m., no matter how prepared I am: "OK, I've already put out my toothpaste and eye cream on the counter. My clean Contigo coffee cup is sitting under the Keurig spout ready to be filled. Tomorrow's outfit is hanging front and center in the closet. My work bag is packed, save for the stuff that I need to grab from the fridge."

Set that alarm for 2:45 a.m., baby!

Other evenings, I'm not so on top of things: "Ah man, I never packed my lunch. My travel mug is still dirty from the morning before, so I'll have to rinse it out before I can make my critical cup at 3 a.m. Shit, I never switched my parking pass out from the other car."

Ugh, OK, the latest I can get away with is 2:37 a.m.

These mental discussions with myself were equal parts exhausting and ridiculous. How many minutes can I add to the alarm for any blissful additional rest? How many minutes must I subtract because I didn't have the energy to get my work bag ready?

Regardless of my actual wake-up call time, I'm still *always* tired. I drag myself into my closet, trying to find coordination to put on my outfit, not trip as I put on my shoes, and pull on the sweatpants I wore under my dress.

At 3:09 a.m., I'm in the car headed to work. Admittedly, I enjoy the quiet commute and chopping the drive time essentially in half. (I've got to be mindful of the drunk drivers, however.) Once I make the loop around the block into the station parking lot, I find the closest spot to the door. By this point, I'm a little more awake, even though I haven't sipped any of the coffee I brewed at 3 a.m. I keep my head up, vigilantly making sure I'm not approached on the dark city street. Then, I stumble my way to the weather office, greet my producer (if I have one that day) with a mutual grumble, and begin the attempt to conceal the growing dark circles under my eyes. Arrive on set camera-ready (and perky, please!) at 4:20 a.m. for mic and camera checks. I'm always late (and grumpy).

Then, it's off to the races for the next five hours with rapid-fire TV weather hits jumping between five different locations in the studio, immediately followed by live radio hits for the morning drive, for which I actually had to run to the whisper booth in order to be on time.

Allow me to describe a space that perhaps sounds

like a glamorous haven. The whisper booth (or radio booth) from which thousands of Philadelphians got their daily weather updates from me is a literal dark hole in the wall. One of those cheap desk lamps that clamps onto the tabletop at least allows me to see the keyboard in front of me. A little TV monitor perched in the upper corner lets me keep an eye on the real-time broadcast. Bonus, I can switch to a channel that shows a quad shot of four field cameras so if it's a nice morning, I can watch a pretty sunrise remotely. But in actuality, that booth is a modest step up from a Port-A-Potty sized cave.

Steve once remarked about my work, "It's like you're in a job interview for five hours every day." What an accurate observation. Live broadcasting can be draining. You have to be "on" all the time, and if you're not, people let you know it.

After the five-hour marathon, my energy typically crashes for two hours before I need to prep for the next show at noon. "OK, girl," I tell myself, "try to be just as perky as you were after that glorious first cup of coffee kicked in. Just power through one more half-hour show, and call it a nine-hour day." Start unhooking the microphone before the show's goodbye music ends. Then speed out the door like a bat out of hell. Get in the car and peel out of there, tires screeching as you careen through the parking lot maze to get out of the electronic gate.

Now to make it through the afternoon. Feel the relief of being done for the day as you maneuver through West Philly's lunch traffic. Make a mental checklist for how you'll productively spend your afternoon: playing with the girls, working out, sitting on the deck if it's a nice afternoon, knocking out a load of laundry and straightening up the walk-in closet which you left looking like a disaster.

Pull into the garage shortly after 1:00 p.m. and greet two sweet, lively toddlers, giving out hugs and kisses. They can't wait to help you make that second cup of coffee you've been craving all morning long. As that brews, race upstairs to change into sweatpants as quickly as possible. (Get me out of these Spanx, STAT!) Your still darkened bedroom, with the blackout shades and curtains drawn, invitingly lures you in for a nap as you stifle a yawn.

I swear to myself that I'll only conk out for an hour. Then 4:30 p.m. rolls around and I've slept away the entire afternoon, along with any chance of checking things off my to-do list. Groggily, I go downstairs and do a whole lot of nothing for the next hour. Then, I make dinner for the girls. We rarely eat as a family at this point, so cue the mommy guilt that sits like a festering cyst in the back corner of my mind.

You see the insanity of this, right?

For a long time, I didn't. But when Steph died, it hit me. I was just trying to get through each week, rarely enjoying each day as it came. I was a literal Loverboy song, "Working for the Weekend."

In the list of reasons why I made the decision to take drastic charge of my own life, Stephanie Bloom is way up at the top. Her life story made me realize once and for all how critical my time here really is.

COULD I DISS THE 2:45 A.M. ALARM?

Steph lived a lot of life in her final, difficult months. She fought for her chance to spend as much time as she possibly could building her relationships and loving her family with the time she had. Despite a tough months-long battle, Steph still found the physical energy to enjoy day trips to the beach, cook Thanksgiving dinner with her family and go to the movie theater to see "The Incredibles."

Then, there was me. I couldn't rally the energy to walk to the playground with my girls. Hell, I'd barely make the 100-step walk to their backyard fort to push them on the swings. I had no energy. I hated myself for it.

Why? Because I knew damn well I didn't want to miss even one moment.

Functioning with only 4-6 hours of sleep per night sucks. It's particularly hard when you're naturally a cranky bitch when you haven't consumed enough caffeine or slept enough.

I totally expected to be exhausted when my girls were born. However, even after the every-three-hour feedings ended, after I stopped breastfeeding, after the girls grew out of pacifiers and we didn't have to go army-crawling for a lost one under their toddler bed at 1:37 a.m., the extreme tiredness didn't go away. I couldn't get a full night's sleep on any weeknight to save my life.

My husband gladly would have taken on the task of putting the girls to bed solo so I could head to bed. But here's the thing. I didn't want to miss that. My girls, like most children, are at their sweetest, snuggliest and cutest right after they wake up well-rested in the morning. I missed those precious early moments five out of seven mornings. So even though bedtime is always more irritable (for all of us!), I couldn't get past the guilt or the disappointment of not participating in that routine with my children.

So, I'd stay up. When babes are small enough, you can still get away with putting them to bed at 7:00 p.m. Now that worked for me. But since I couldn't freeze time and keep them in that routine, the girls began staying up later and later. My wakeup time never changed, but my window of rest kept shrinking. Despite my best exhaustion-driven efforts to engage with my family, I couldn't devote the part of me I wanted to be fully present.

Even though other things chipped away at my resolve to stick out my situation, I figured I'd made my bed, so now I must lay in it. Plus, the practical implications of making a change were insurmountable in my narrow mind. My husband loved the area and didn't want to leave. I worked in a business niche with non-compete agreements where to change companies, I'd have to uproot my family and move. I felt totally stuck.

As more workplace frustrations continued to crop up—squashed attempts to grow professionally, stupid office drama, the feeling of being unappreciated, and that damn ever-present 2:45 a.m. alarm—my professional discontent mounted. Crushing me. Eventually, the bad outweighed the good and it was time to fix it.

There's a vital question we should all answer. I'm willing to bet it's one that you can answer in an instant.

Quick! Don't think! Just answer: What matters most to you? Is it family? Your work? The ability to lead a joyful, peaceful, healthy and content life?

It's all of those things for me.

Whether you lead a charmed life or like most of us, have struggles to overcome, your approach to it makes all the difference. Circumstance, fate and things we just didn't plan for will befall us all. You might lose your job. You might have to uproot your family due to a natural disaster. A loved one might get deployed. You might have to take on the responsibility of caring for an aging relative. Your spouse might get sick, or your child, or you.

But how you work with the hand you're dealt doesn't only say so much about the kind of person you are. With the right mindset, you actually can handle anything that gets thrown your way. And you can live a life full of meaning and joy.

Steph sure as hell did. Sweet, strong Steph.

She left us on October 3, 2018.

Almost exactly one year later, I took a leap and made a drastic life change.

3
THE MENTAL SHIFT

❝ To be yourself in a world that is constantly trying to make you something else is the greatest accomplishment."

— RALPH WALDO EMERSON

❝ Self-awareness is probably the most important thing toward being a champion."

— BILLIE JEAN KING

When I was a toddler, playing quietly in my room one day, I sprinkled talcum powder all over my rug. As any parent will tell you, a toddler playing noiselessly in another room can mean bad things, so my mother came to check on me. As she opened the bedroom door, she got hit with a cloud of powder. As my mother relates the story, I stood, innocently wide-eyed in the middle of the huge mess.

"Why did you pour powder all over the rug?" she understandably wanted to know.

"Because I wanted to make footprints," I proudly replied, little puffs of powder popping off my lips, my mother fighting back the urge to howl with laughter.

My mom loves this story. She even told it as part of a beautiful speech she gave at my wedding rehearsal dinner. She beamed with maternal pride at all the "footprints" I'd made with my accomplishments ever since that fateful day with the talcum powder: my stint as a professional musician, my aspiration to become a TV personality and my resolve to go back to school to become a meteorologist. She described how proud she was of the "imprint" I was creating on my future husband's heart. It was such a touching tribute and makes me cry every time I rewatch our wedding video.

But here's the thing: While those accomplishments were definitely something to be proud of, they weren't necessarily the product of any personal dream fulfillment.

No. Much of what I could tout as "life accomplishments" is actually me making floundering attempts to catch my own white whale, my elusive dream of a perfect, actualized existence. It's true: I've accrued a pretty vast repertoire of professional work. I've taken up a lot of hobbies. I've instilled many personal habits. All this, with the hope of achieving pure bliss. But that bleached behemoth representing my idyllic personal existence? Despite all that trial and error, I never found it.

But I finally figured out why—an unfortunate trifecta of shiny object syndrome, outside influence and competence (despite my insecurities). That's how I ended up here.

REACH FOR THE STARS

As a kid, I wanted to grow up to be a pediatrician or a veterinarian. When I was learning those words, I couldn't quite put those syllables together correctly. So when I proudly announced my future ambitions to my aunt, you'll forgive her confusion that my 4-year-old life's dream was to be a "pedestrian" or a "vegetarian." At other points in my childhood, I also wanted to be a rock star, a movie star, a fashion designer, a marine biologist and a teacher.

I dreamed big and wanted to experiment, to try everything. As children, we're told that we can be anything we want to be. Want to be an astronaut? Reach for the stars! Have a burning motivation to become president of the United States? Yes, you can! Busting your butt to become a pro ball player? Work hard enough and you'll knock it out of the park!

I gravitated to this idea. However, while inspiration like this is vital for kids, it had an unintended flip side for me. Telling little indecisive Katie that she can be anything she sets her mind to gave me way too many options. I saw a lot of shiny, beautiful, appealing-at-face-value options. I wanted to do them all.

One of my few regrets was not having structured guidance to figure out my path before I started college. I didn't know what I wanted to do with my life after high school. I *thought* I knew, but no. I mean, I loved music. I taught myself to play piano at age 9, played the flute and piccolo through my senior year, sang in every choral group available, and even landed a few leadership roles in band. The obvious choice? Study music education and performance.

As it turns out, music was a great hobby, and I actually worked at it professionally through several paying gigs as an accompanist, soloist, and wedding and church musician. I even lasted through two-and-a-half years of music as my college major. Something just wasn't feeling right about it, so I transferred schools halfway through my college stint. Then, I realized the school wasn't the problem, it was the major. At that point, I didn't know where I should end up, so I took core classes at my local community college until I could figure out my next move.

Then one Sunday, a woman at my church approached me about an internship opportunity. To this day, I don't know what made her think of me. I had yet to settle on communications as a major. But she told me there was a chance to intern at RCN 4 in Bath, PA, a tiny broadcasting station that produced a daily, pre-recorded six-minute newscast.

A chance to learn the TV ropes? Sounded cool to me. Was I actually interested in it as a career? Hell if I knew. But why not? I applied, and got the gig. This internship was amazing. As I'd learn later, most TV stations, especially in the higher markets, don't let interns use, let alone touch, any equipment. Acquired hands-on experience turned into my resume gold.

One day, I ran the audio board for the actual

newscast. I honed my pathetic writing skills and helped the executive producer (who also anchored the show) write some of the stories. The station even let me do a package series about summer wedding planning. I also tried my hand at anchoring the news one evening.

Those segments actually aired on local television. It was unheard of demo reel material. Most college kids only get a chance to put some amateur campus-studio material on a reel for their first job. But there I was, a gal with a leg up simply because I had legitimate material that ran on real airwaves to submit to my eventual first boss.

Those examples weren't the regular day-to-day routine, however. My role at the small station primarily included accompanying the chief photographer out on stories that would be part of that evening's newscast. We'd make two or three stops to shoot B-roll, ask a few questions, and be on our way. The stories we covered were beyond boring, to me, anyway. Press conferences for local representatives and district attorneys, or some event at a local park, and of course, the perp walks.

I learned during this internship exactly what a perp walk is. It's short for perpetrator walk: The alleged perpetrator of a crime literally walks down or across a hall to meet with lawyers or to be taken to a jail cell. We always had to rush and get ourselves situated, because even though the perp walk might be 25 minutes in the future, camera crews and reporters never knew when, so we always had to be ready to roll.

I despised the hurry-up-and-wait cadence, the pressure of the deadlines and the rigor of working in the field. Of course, I never let on how much I disliked it. Deep down, I didn't think this was for me, but I didn't want to let down the people who'd given me a chance. The result? I allowed others to dictate how my life should look, a surefire path to ending up doing something that wasn't right for me.

Here's what I learned much later: Your personal path to fulfillment is a tough thing to figure out and actualize when you're an appeaser, a people-pleaser. When you act the way you think "they" want you to, you stray far off your destined path.

YOUR OPINION MATTERS MOST

For so long, I didn't work, do or live for myself. As far back as I can remember, I've fallen back on this unfortunate personality trait of letting everyone else's opinions outweigh my own, like 90% of the time. The consequence of all that outside influence, all those people's ideas of how my life should look, led me down a career path that wasn't personally fulfilling.

You know the saying: "Opinions are like assholes and they all stink." There's definitely a partial truth there. Sure, there are a lot of bogus opinions flying around, but not all of them are bad. Plenty of well-intentioned people have told me what they thought I should do. My mother thought I should revamp my music background and try to rebuild a presence as a professional soloist or accompanist. My husband suggested that I try out for a backup anchor spot to broaden my skill set. The difference with these examples? They happened recently, after I'd settled my mind on what I did and didn't want. When my mother and husband made these suggestions, I knew immediately, with zero question or hesitation, that I didn't want to do those things at all.

It feels strange to say that I couldn't think for myself for a long time, in both huge, life-altering choices to the most miniscule. Think I'm exaggerating? Once I drank a Coke that my date had ordered for me with dinner, even though I hate soda. I forced it down just because he liked it.

This is classic "Coming to America" stuff, right? Remember when Eddie Murphy's character, the crown prince of Zamunda, meets his betrothed Imani Izzi for the first time?

"What do you like to do?" Prince Akeem asks, as casually as possible, given the awkward situation.

"Whatever you like," she says, as she bows to him.

"What kind of music do you like?" he asks, more specifically.

"Whatever kind of music you like," she lilts, again with the bow.

With slight frustration, Prince Akeem explains that he understands Imani has been trained to serve him and like everything he likes, but he'd like to understand who she is as a person.

"Do you have a favorite food?" he asks Imani, hoping for a third-time's-the-charm outcome.

"Yes!" she affirms with a sweet smile.

"Good!" Akeem exclaims, encouraged. "What is your favorite food?"

"Whatever food you like," she bows again.

Facepalm to the forehead. Ugh. I mean, I give credit to Prince Akeem for wanting to get to know Imani. But, why oh why, hierarchical class systems aside, do we let anybody else dictate our interests, our preferences or our dreams?

I think the answer is simple, but overcoming it is extremely difficult.

It's insecurity.

Letting someone else's preference decide your beverage choice is one thing. But far more damaging is letting someone else's ideas control how your life should turn out.

When I took voice lessons, I was told that I was halfway decent at performing classical and operatic vocal pieces, so I steered clear of the more current musical genres I preferred. When I pitched a franchise of news magazine-style stories about weather's impact on everyday lifestyle, my supervisor told me he liked me better in the news role. Again, I begrudgingly steered myself away from doing the feature reporting I preferred, thinking, "Yeah, I guess he's right."

For far too long, I was entirely malleable. Sure, I had my own ideas of what I wanted, but when the opportunity came to express those ideas to anyone else, I'd give in to their assumptions or grand thoughts of what I'd be good at and what path I should take. Eventually, I began to rely almost solely on what other people told me to do. My voice went silent.

Others' opinions, even if they come from a place of good intentions, should never rule your life. As a disclaimer, of course, you should seek guidance, absorb advice and take practicality into account over your decisions. But you can't lose yourself in the discussion. Your opinion matters most when it's your life in question.

Quite often, a career path that's based around your strengths will make you happy. But it's totally possible to use that same powerful skill set doing something successfully that you don't enjoy. I was pretty good at what ended up becoming my career for so long, so I kept going. In fact, as it turned out, I kept getting lucky. Or, at least, I kept performing well enough and working hard enough that I landed job after job in the TV business.

I HAD THE JOB 'EVERYONE WANTED'

In my first real job out of school, I was a reporter and producer at the local PBS station close to home. It was a 9-to-5, weekends-off job, a luxury in TV when you're just starting out. My role was to produce, write and report long-form packages for a news-magazine show. However, it wasn't the right fit for me for a lot of reasons, mostly because the day-to-day reporting and producing of these stories left me stressed out and fatigued.

I didn't love the rigor of lugging gear to and from locations. I didn't love five-hour field shoots that left me sore and sweaty. I didn't love having to try to look presentable for my on-camera standups via a news van rear-view mirror, working by uneven light. I didn't love how disorganized I became because I carted half my desk around in a bag. I was decent at it, but it just wasn't my wheelhouse.

As I approached the two-year mark at this organization, I needed to move on to a new opportunity.

I applied for several hosting positions, none of which ever called me. Then one day, I saw a listing for a video broadcaster position at AccuWeather. I thought to myself, "Weather? Do I even have the skill set to pull that off?" I'd never stood in front of, let alone actually worked with, a green screen. I didn't have a meteorology degree at this point, and the job also meant moving away from my family for the first time in my life.

And yet, I was intrigued. The listing said, "Meteorology degree preferred, not required." So they're willing to train, huh? I showed the listing to a close friend, who immediately said, "You have to go for this. You'd be fantastic at it." He always managed to see the potential in me that I couldn't see in myself.

I went for it. Nearly six years later, my resume tape was full of live hits I'd done for a dozen different national and regional networks and on-location reports from major weather events. I now had experience in radio, in leading my own franchise (both with a video segment on climate change and weather's impact on sports), and leadership experience developing onboarding training for new employees.

By this point, I'd also surrounded myself with the best and most supportive group of friends I'd ever known. I'd grown to love living in rural central Pennsylvania. I'd also met and gotten engaged to Steve, the love of my life. Sure, I had frustrations at work, but the good still far outweighed the bad.

Then, I got headhunted. The vice president overseeing all the CBS owned-and-operated stations nationwide emailed me about a weekend meteorologist position at the CBS station in New York City. I was totally floored. He'd seen one of my national hits and was impressed. What else could I do? "You just don't say no to that opportunity," my brain told me matter-of-factly. I went to the Big Apple for an interview and landed the job.

This is what I was supposed to want, right? A job in the number one market in the country. The opportunity to pass Katie Couric, Boomer Esiason or Nate Berkus in the hall. The status of having keycard access to the CBS Broadcast Center on West 57th Street. A dedicated room for hair and makeup and pro artists staffed to help with both. This was the feeling of really having made it in this business.

But as I accepted this new role, uprooted my future husband from Happy Valley and moved into a new life that should have felt exciting, I was terrified I'd made a mistake. Before I even started my job, things didn't feel right. Suddenly, I had a 90-minute commute each way on weekdays. I'd be in a large, bustling city every day when I preferred the countryside's quiet and rolling hills. This job took me away from my friends. I also had to go back to the field reporting I so strongly disliked three days a week.

Even though my gut told me this wasn't what I wanted, my brain overrode it and said, "Do you know how many people would kill to be in your shoes? You'd better suck it up and deal, Crazy Pants! This is your chance! This is *the* chance! Cool it with the doubt and buck up!"

This job was what I was supposed to want. And so I pretended I did.

My New York City gig lasted slightly longer than a New York minute. I was there all of five months before the next job opening came calling: the role as the main morning meteorologist at our sister station in Philadelphia. For a variety of reasons, this didn't feel right either. Just like in New York, you can't take off three solid, specific months out of the year because of sweeps. As a staple of the morning show, you can't have any semblance of a normal 9-5 job. All of this comes with the territory. Sure, you'll have weekends off, but you'll have to wake up against your body's natural rhythm in the middle of the night, five out of seven days. If you ever get sick, someone else's schedule will get royally screwed up to cover for you. (I felt crippling guilt anytime I had to call out for an illness.)

But I had the job opportunity that "everyone wanted."

When you graduate with a degree in communications or journalism, the assumed goal is that you'll work your way from small-town, small-market sectors or publications to top-market or national audiences. Shouldn't I want that, too? I mean, I got to be on TV! I got to broadcast my voice and image and influence to thousands of listeners and viewers five days a week! I got to dress up in pretty dresses every day, with full HD makeup and coiffed hair! A former colleague said it best, "It's like getting dressed up to attend a wedding every day of the week."

At face value, I got paid to hang out with my morning team on the daily and crack jokes on the air. I could partake in bits like taste-testing the newest Oreo flavor on set. Yeah, there were parts of my job that I adored. I had the sincere privilege to work with broadcast legends, and to call these people not just colleagues, but friends.

And the actual work: I love the spontaneity of live TV, the off-the-cuff banter and the opportunity to inform people what they can expect and how it'll impact their day. I'm comfortable and at home hooked up to a mic with an ominous robotic camera on me or wearing a set of bulky headphones with a shock-mounted, wind-screened condenser mic all up in my personal oral space. At its core, I adored the most basic parts of my gig. Believe me, it was confusing to feel so miserable when I actually enjoyed the fundamental tenets of what I chose to do every day.

MY BIG 4

Now that I can step outside myself and look at my career as a whole, I've definitely spent the bulk of it doing things I'm good at. You simply don't get opportunities like working at the network level or the chance to remain this long in market number four or above without some skill and natural ability. I certainly never had anything handed to me.

But here too, and for so long, I let insecurity creep in, believing I was just lucky to get those chances, not necessarily that the work I'd put in earned it. I convinced myself that with every network live hit or ad-libbed ad nauseum repetition of a forecast, the work experience I tucked under my belt made me fortunate because someone gave me the chance, rather than the fact that damn it, I deserved the opportunity. Having spent enough time in a business that's extremely hard to break into, let alone thrive in, I now appreciate that this "broadcasting thing" is, in fact, one of my strengths.

However, I wasn't using this strength in a way that brought me joy. I had a life that looked great on paper. When you peel away what you saw on just my CV, there was a lot missing. And although I was starting to really grasp that I needed a new path, I had no clue how else I could use this skill set. If not an on-air meteorologist, what else would I possibly do?

I started an intense self-audit, trying to understand myself. Over the course of hours, days, weeks and eventually months, I sat quietly contemplating who I wanted to be, what I wanted to do and the imprint I wanted to leave on this world. I thought long and extremely hard about all the reasons I've described: about why I couldn't or didn't feel like I could settle on the answers to these important questions. Why couldn't I go after something that would actually fulfill me? As I got in my head, I realized there was one main reason I'd never change without serious resolve and serious action.

It goes back to fear. However, scared as I was, I knew I had reached my breaking point. It was time for a change and I had to figure this out.

There was no other option now.

I had come across a very simple written exercise that gave me a place to start. The idea? You list out the Big 4: the four things in your life that, when combined together, will bring you total happiness. I had nothing to lose, so I tried it. Pen and notebook at the ready, I sat on my bed one afternoon and thought meticulously about what four facets of life could bring me a life of fulfillment.

I started by writing down the broadest bullet points of the kind of person I wanted to be, my overall end game.

So what were they? To quote "Miracle on 34th Street," they're "kindness and joy and love and all the other intangibles." (Don't get it twisted, Fred Gailey, my Christmas movie quote game is sick.) But that really is what it boils down to if I'm defining what would make me happy in the most generalized terms.

In my happiest place, I'd be:

- A kinder human
- A more joyful worker and parent
- A more loving spouse and friend.

To reiterate Mr. Gailey, "Don't overlook those lovely intangibles. You'll discover those are the only things that are worthwhile."

That part of the exercise was easy to complete. I want to live a kinder, more joyful and loving life. Now, how would I get there? I commenced brainstorming. I talked to myself out loud, coached myself through each idea that came to me and took this seriously. Safe to say, my notebook contained a lot of chicken scratch by the end. I wrote a lot of ideas, crossed them off, rewrote them, circled them and scribbled them out again.

Finally, I settled on "My Big 4 Keys to Happy." Here's what I concluded.

To actualize what happiness means for me, I need these four things:

1. Freedom, to make my own schedule and my own choices, and to have total control over my own life
2. Creativity, and to have outlets for it, whether it's via content creation, DIY projects or some other medium
3. Personal growth, so I can develop as a human and a professional
4. Relationships, since my interactions with family, friends and business partners come first and I must be able to foster them.

It's pretty mainstream stuff, I'd say. There's nothing about this that's at all revolutionary. Understand though, for me, this was a mind blow. I had lived for so many years doing what everyone else thought I should do. I set myself up to take life as it had been handed to me. "Welp, I guess this is the best it's going to get," I'd say to myself. "I'll have to settle and live out my time just getting through one day at a time."

This realization kicked my brain into high gear and

I began to believe I could, in fact, change my situation. Hope was starting to glimmer.

And then something magical occurred.

FUEL FOR THE FIRE

Shortly after the Big 4 exercise, I saw an Audible ad while I browsed on Amazon. I never was a huge fan of audio books, since I preferred to read the words myself. But there was a deal to get your first book free. Besides, Yacht Rock on SiriusXM was getting a little worn out for my early morning listening pleasure, and I needed more content to consume for the commute. So I thought, what the hell, I'll give it a try.

I decided to download "Girl, Stop Apologizing" by Rachel Hollis. Up until then, I'd never been a self-help, motivational content seeker. I'd heard of Hollis and knew of her work, but I'm almost exclusively a fiction gal. I'm not even sure what made me settle on this book, but I started listening.

If there was any ounce of doubt about what I needed to do, that book was all the motivation I needed to squash it. Listening to Hollis' hilarious stories and sage wisdom got me pumped. "Girl, Stop Apologizing" wasn't the reason I decided it was finally time to make a change, but it was the fuel I needed to throw on the little fire I was tending in my gut. I had it burning pretty well, good enough to toast a few marshmallows. But Hollis' words were like throwing gasoline on that shit, I got so fired up (pardon the pun).

I remember my eyes welling up at one particular section. Picture this: I'm driving down City Avenue in Philadelphia at 3:17 a.m., intently paying attention, my eyes on the road and my ears on Rachel's voice. I'm relating so deeply to her words as she talks about limiting beliefs and excuses that hold us back. Then she says something that brought the whole thing home: "It's time to stop apologizing for who you are. It's time to become who you were made to be."

Rachel. Girl. You get it.

That was it. Right there. That line, that was it. Become who you were made to be.

I wasn't made for this. I wasn't made for my current situation. I wasn't made to be OK with not knowing until two weeks out whether I'd be granted time off on Christmas morning to be with my family. I wasn't made to feel exhilarating excitement when breaking news or major storm coverage kept us on the air wall-to-wall, working 12-hour shifts with short turnaround to the next exhausting day. Much as I'd like, I wasn't made with the ability to hang through an entire Philadelphia Union night match when I'm dog-tired (despite determinedly chugging coffee at 4 p.m.).

Making matters more volatile, I'm a human who

comes equipped with reasons to be pissy. Straight out of the box, I'm a classic Cancer crab, moody as shit. And since having children, my premenstrual hormones rage off the friggin' charts. On top of it all, I was always tired. ALWAYS.

I knew what I didn't want. A big first step, but I still had a lot of work to do and a lot of very important questions to answer. Chief among them, what *was* I made for? And how the hell do I turn it into reality?

It's a difficult process, figuring all this out, especially since most of us don't have a road map to follow. Sorting out your own Big 4 may help. What kind of person do you want to be? What traits would the happiest version of you possess?

Next, assess what things you need in your life to help you become the most joyful version of you. Check in with yourself during the day and notice when you feel that bliss. Are you doing certain activities? Are you in the company of certain people? Pay attention to when you're exuberant. Then, write down the qualities in your own life that bring you fulfillment and happiness.

You know mine: freedom, creativity, personal growth and relationships. Maybe your Big 4 overlap with or echo mine. Maybe none do. Maybe words like connection, health, mindset, beauty, nature, learning or heritage resonate with you. There are plenty more. Consider many, and then narrow them down to four.

Once you've settled on your Big 4—the four keys to your unique personal happiness— you can begin the physical work toward actualizing it.

But it has to start in your head.

4

THE ACTIVE SHIFT

> The only way to do great work is to love what you do. If you haven't found it yet, keep looking. Don't settle. As with all matters of the heart, you'll know when you find it."
>
> — STEVE JOBS

Freedom, creativity, personal growth and relationships—I had a mental jumping-off point, my Big 4 keys to my personal happiness. Now, I needed to break this down into action items. I asked myself in the most general of terms: What could I do every single day that would bring me joy for the rest of my life? What won't I get tired of? What won't I lose interest in? What would sustain me for the long haul? I still like the actual work I do, so do I just need to find a new company? Do I need to change cities? Do I need a different kind of role in TV?

Or is the job fine and I just need distractions?

So many daunting, big questions swirled in my mind. Taking actual steps toward change was even more intimidating. But I knew that couldn't keep me from starting.

Sean Cannell, one of my favorite influencers in the YouTube video creation space, put it perfectly: "Start. Start now. Start where you are. Start with what you have. Start with all your insecurities. Start with what you already know. Start moving toward the goal. Start and make mistakes. Start small. Start now."

We all have to start somewhere. You've already read some of the roadblocks I faced on this journey. Peeps, we're merely scratching the surface. The mental indecision I've described, the lack of self-worth, along with the sheer and constant exhaustion. Pfft. Honey, we're just getting started.

There are—and will be—so many hoops you'll need to jump through, so many pep talks you'll need to give yourself to keep going, and so much negativity you'll need to tune out to reach your potential, and ultimately, your happiest and healthiest existence.

I went back to the idea of distractions. That seemed like a path of minimal resistance. I gave in to the notion that I just needed something extracurricular to keep me occupied—a hobby or activity I could look forward to losing myself in for a little while to decompress and lift my mood.

Over several years, I worked at this devotedly.

DISTRACTION ATTEMPT #1: FAIL

I started with fitness. I knew I needed to get into better shape and hoped I could use endorphins, greater overall health and better-fitting jeans to propel me into a happier mindset.

This was an unfortunate multi-year "exercise" with too-high expectations. Dude, I gave everything a shot.

I tried to wake up 10 minutes early to crank out some core exercise for a while. I couldn't sustain giving up that sleep.

I tried working out immediately upon stepping foot into the house after work. I was just too damn tired.

I tried to motivate myself with at-home programs that took the guesswork out of what I should do on any given day. I couldn't keep up with the schedule.

I tried joining a gym that held late afternoon classes. That worked for a while. Then I got pregnant with twins. For the good of the little beans growing inside me, I scaled my strenuous activity way back, but couldn't work with the gym schedule once the girls were born. Two babies nurse a lot. So I gave up entirely.

After so many failed attempts to build a fitness habit, I finally plopped down exasperatedly to assess what kept holding me back. By this point, experience had taught me a few things. If I joined another gym, I'd need to go immediately after work with the late lunch crowd. I knew I wouldn't be able to step foot in my house first because I'd never have the discipline to schlep back out again for high-impact workouts. I knew I wanted a facility that offered some version or variety of my favorite classes: yoga, boot camp and spin. The problem? The convenient gyms only offered morning and evening classes, not early afternoon sessions when I wanted to attend.

However, I enjoyed a stroke of fortune when I stumbled on a gym that offered yoga classes at 12:45 p.m. Better yet, the facility was on the ground floor of our office building. I could haul ass from the time the noon show ended at 12:27 p.m. to change out of my on-air gear and into stretchy pants, run out to the parking lot to grab my mat from my trunk, and then race down the block, all with enough time to get a decent spot on the floor and catch my breath before the instructor turned on the chill music and led the group into child's pose.

But sadly, I got lazy again, stopped attending regularly, and eventually the classes moved earlier, so I couldn't go anyway.

DISTRACTION ATTEMPT #2: FAIL

I tried losing myself in literature and rekindled a steamy relationship with my local library.

As a kid, my trips to the Allentown Public Library were one of my favorite things to do. My mother and I would split up when we got there. She'd stay downstairs browsing the fiction titles, while I excitedly rode the elevator one floor up to the children's section. I don't know if they're still there, but back in the '80s, the Allentown branch had these giant, round pod-style lounge chairs in the kids' section. They were mid-century modern in bright shades of orange, white and black, all of which clashed with the carpet's brown-and-mustard print. I always thought these retro-futuristic chairs looked like gigantic Reese's Pieces sitting haphazardly in the middle of the room.

As I moved around over the years, I kept up my reading hobby for a time. I give credit to the Bethlehem Area Public Library for my introduction to the Harry Potter series. Later, thanks to the Schlow Centre Region Library in State College, I devoured Agatha Christie novels on the regular and read all 1000 pages of "Gone with the Wind" (a feat I'd always wanted to check off my bucket list). But somewhere along the way, I just stopped. No reason, no rhyme. I just didn't go to the library anymore.

Thankfully, a serendipitous coincidence occurred as I cared for my tiny twins. The constant chasing, checking, changing, catching, racing, rushing, feeding and fatigue-inducing marathon meant I could never settle into any activity that required focus for very long. I could barely bring myself to leave them alone for five minutes while I showered, I had so many first-time parent nerves. I was getting tired of constantly scrolling on my smartphone and needed an activity I could stop and start easily. So, after a nearly five-year abandonment of a lifelong hobby, I packed up my tiny family one afternoon. I staunchly rolled my double stroller into my local library and applied for a new library card (and got one for each of my girls while I was at it—turns out, you can carry a library card even at the tender age of 1).

From there, I read my way through all the Ruth Ware and Gillian Flynn psychothrillers, all the complex relationships in Liane Moriarty's work and every book that Reese Witherspoon recommended. As a personal regressive tactic, I started working my way through the entire Nancy Drew collection. And it helped. I did get lost in the stories as I plowed through two or three books every month for a while.

I developed a new routine of using my between-shows hour to walk the half-mile to the nearest Starbucks on Callowhill Street in Philadelphia with my latest find from the Delaware County Library System, and pick up my grande hazelnut dark roast in a venti cup. I'd make my way to the closest public seating area to read as many pages as I could before making the trek back to the station to primp and prep for the noon show. For a while, I loved sitting by the fountains at the Barnes Foundation, a few short additional steps past the coffee shop. I later switched it up and retraced my steps to read at the little park next to the Community College of Philadelphia. This was usually a bustling spot, with lots of people walking dogs, nannies pushing baby strollers, seniors getting exercise and students killing time between classes. But by the end of a particularly damp summer, the mosquitoes ran rampant and I, being a prime target, would get back to the station with at least five or six fresh bug bites.

Still, I found a refuge in reading. Any avid reader knows the joy you find between the pages of a book. Someone once said that reading is dreaming with your eyes wide open. I escaped my frustrated reality with these characters whenever I flipped open my latest borrowed find. Even the physical volumes themselves brought me comfort. I get nostalgic satisfaction when I inhale the slightly musty scent of the pages and crinkle the plastic protective cover.

But when I had to put the book down and walk back to the TV station or turn off my reading light before sunset in my blacked-out bedroom because I had to wake in the middle of the night, I settled right back into my familiar irritation and misery. It was a worthy effort. I still read a lot, but it just wasn't enough.

DISTRACTION ATTEMPT #3: FAIL

Given my lifelong love for all things DIY, I naturally dove headfirst into making Pinterest-worthy memories for my daughters.

Through trying to curate the coolest, happiest and most special childhood ever for these girls, I was reenacting or creating experiences I adored as a child myself or wish I had. I put on over-the-top themed birthday parties for them every summer with handcrafted party games, themed menu items and decor. I meticulously curated homemade family photo albums each year. I planned Mommy-and-me getaways every summer with each daughter. I designed an intricately detailed Advent calendar to count down the days until Christmas with special activities to do all month long. Special campouts in the backyard, little treasure hunts around the house, you name it, I did it.

Of course, along the way, I documented our adventures on social media—partly because I enjoyed sharing them and getting people's kind feedback, and also because it was part of my job and public persona. I received so many sweet compliments: "You're creating such wonderful memories for your daughters." "They'll never forget this." "What a great mom you are!" "Supermom! How do you do it?!"

But truly, I jam-packed the girls' days with stuff to do, in part so I'd have something else to focus on. Toiling at projects that benefited my girls meant I could lose myself in the distraction of the latest spray paint job, the newest Pinterest board to create or the next overnight trip to plan. Yes, I absolutely adored spending time on these things. Of course as a mother, you derive pleasure from your children's happiness. But was that the sole reason I did it all? Absolutely not. And yes, having a nearly obsessive, over-the-top hobby to cultivate gave me things to look forward to, for a while.

Here I come again with my dead horse to beat. It was still painful to walk into work in the dead of night. I began to feel physical dread when I arrived at the parking lot, literally slowing to a heavy plod when I stepped out of my car to walk the 300 steps to the elevator. While I loved surfing the web for DIY party favors, mapping out the December calendar's festive daily activities or creating "What to Pack" lists for one of our mom-and-daughter getaways to a Pocono mountain cabin, my attempt to be the perfect Pinterest mom wasn't enough to quench my own need for self-satisfaction.

Another quality attempt had failed.

IS A RADICAL 180 THE ANSWER?

I was beyond frustrated that I couldn't figure this out. I didn't believe I had any other option but to distract myself into happiness. And I certainly didn't believe that I could possibly do anything else professionally with the skill set I had.

With a narrow viewpoint, I thought I was doomed to work unfavorable schedules for the rest of my professional career. What else can a professional with bachelor's degrees in communications and meteorology do but work as a TV meteorologist?

A switch finally clicked in my head when I figured it wouldn't hurt to see what else might be out there for me to do with my life.

I began to research.

I began to read.

I began to watch videos.

I began to follow more and more influencers and entrepreneurs.

I began to realize my self-imposed view of what I was capable of was insanely short-sighted. There are a ton of ways I could profitably use my skill set. I have killer organization skills. I'm a natural at this whole broadcasting and production thing. I love the creative and editorial process. I enjoy public speaking and working in the spotlight.

What if I started a list of pursuits I could channel these skills into?

I could run a production company. I could become a blogger on all things video production or DIY. I could open a video production school to teach aspiring creators. I could open an Etsy shop and sell my DIY creations. I could work as a freelance field producer. I could develop online DIY courses. I could start a consulting firm and develop content for businesses and brands. I could do affiliate marketing in both the DIY and production realms.

These were outside-the-box ideas compared to what I currently did for a living. However, there was one path that stood out to me, one that led me incredibly close to actually pulling a complete, radical 180.

Mere weeks after Steph passed away, one of the reporters at my station did a feature story. I had just wrapped a live hit for our sister radio station and had popped in my ifb, the little earpiece through which you hear the broadcast and the producers and director can communicate with you. My friend reported about a local DIY workshop.

I was transfixed. I was glued to the story on my muted little monitor, hanging on through my earpiece to every detail of the workshop owner's amazing story. She had been a nurse, but loved crafting and creating, and stumbled upon this cool franchise opportunity. She quit her job and followed a dream to be a business owner working in a niche market for which she had true passion. The rest was history, and here she was—featured on the local news.

I immediately started Googling, right there in the radio booth.

In the short weeks that followed, I hopped on calls with three different franchisors and licensors with similar businesses, discussing opportunities in the greater Philadelphia area. I dove headfirst into reading a several hundred-page franchise disclosure document.

Yes, I convinced myself I should open my own DIY crafting studio. Eventually, however, I talked myself out of it. I remembered my Big 4: freedom, creativity, personal growth and relationships. I needed to keep my eye on those prizes. Opening a workshop meant I could only check off three, but not all four, of those boxes.

From my Big 4, I'd check off creativity, no question.

I'd immerse myself in nail guns, acrylic paint, unfinished wood and stencils. I'd most definitely check off the personal growth box. I'd never built my own business and would have so much to learn. I'd tick off half of the relationships box. There'd certainly be an opportunity for me to build business relationships with a pursuit like this. However, I'd have to work a lot of weekends, likely miss out on some of the girls' stuff, whether they eventually had soccer matches or recitals. I knew without a doubt I'd be so deep in the trenches of running the workshop that I'd skip out on time with my friends.

Could I accept that as a new reality? I was *almost* willing. Anything had to be better than what I was currently doing, I rationalized. I'd get to wake up with my circadian rhythm. But remember, there's still one box to check here.

Freedom.

For weeks, my husband and I went over and over this decision. We were in near daily discussions about how to make something give in my current reality. We were rationally talking about how a huge decision like leaving my TV career would affect us, and it was starting to feel real—and very scary. I tried to put myself in the shoes of what my day-to-day life would look like if I became a DIY workshop owner.

I spoke with and emailed multiple franchisees who

were already making it happen. They were incredibly gracious, explaining what a day in the life of a DIY workshop owner looked like. These ladies kept it real, explaining that a lot of my day would, in fact, be devoted to business tasks like bookkeeping and customer service. Though it was a bit of a buzzkill to hear those accounts compared to what I imagined—days spent experimenting with chunky yarn and staining woodworking projects—I was still excited at the prospect.

Then I spoke to one more workshop owner. She too was open and honest about the joys of owning a business, but she was also blatantly truthful about the reality of the grunt work. Her bluntness talked me out of the venture: "You'll give up weekends. You'll miss stuff—a lot of stuff—with your kids and your family. You won't be home for dinner most nights in the beginning. You'll work 10-hour days until your machine is well-oiled. And you may start to resent it."

It was hard to hear, but I took those words to heart.

Freedom. Wasn't that what I wanted? I revisited my self-audit.

OK, I knew for certain that I wanted to make my own hours and structure my life on my terms. How could I possibly do that when so many facets of this venture worked against that very notion? And by freedom, I also wanted financial freedom. I didn't need to hit it rich, but I did need to be comfortable on a daily basis, without worrying whether we could afford that Grubhub order or if I needed to check my bank account before I paid a bill. There was simply no way to make that happen with this model.

The upfront costs of renting a retail location, plus franchise or licensing fees was enough to worry me. Even though I'd be in charge of the business, I needed to ensure steady cash flow to keep the doors open and pay rent. That meant hosting a constant stream of workshops. If I wanted to take a vacation, I'd have to hire staff. In theory, I'd become stuck in a grind in my own business.

Yeah, that wasn't gonna work.

ALL FOUR BOXES: CHECKED

I remember a conversation Steve and I had one evening after we tucked in the girls for the night. Though he's my number one supporter in everything, he wisely continued to force practicality into the conversation as he took a good look at our finances.

"I ran the numbers while you were at work," he said. He explained the harsh reality that in effect, we'd have to drain our savings to get my dream of a DIY workshop off the ground with zero guarantee of its success.

"I'm terrified," he admitted. His concern deflated

me. With tears welling, I almost wailed, "I can't keep doing this!"

If not this solution, what then? I had put so much research and effort into the idea of my own crafting studio. In that moment, a mix of fatigue, sadness and defeat made me feel as though I'd exhausted my options. But Steve was right. We couldn't dump thousands of our hard-saved nest egg into a pipe dream that, once I was honest about it, wasn't even my true path to happiness.

There's an adage in business: "Cheap, fast and good. Pick two. If it's good and fast, it won't be cheap. If it's cheap and good, it won't be fast. If it's fast and cheap, it won't be good." At least from the perspective of client and business interaction, there's truth in this. But I challenge the philosophy when it comes to achieving personal fulfillment. I believe it's possible to check off all the boxes of what you desire and need to be happy. There had to be a path for me to find total joy. I just needed to find it.

That's why I constantly reminded myself of my Big 4 end game: freedom, creativity, personal growth and relationships. I started brainstorming again. What could I do that would allow me to be there for my family on my terms, create the lifestyle I craved, help me build passive income and maintain a public persona? I continued narrowing down the possibilities, this time with a newfound understanding of what I needed as a professional and as a human.

A light bulb finally went off.

YouTube.

Why not marry my favorite hobby of crafting and creating with my love of content creation into a project I controlled 100 percent? Perfect.

When I started my Katie Fehlinger DIY YouTube channel, I didn't have a clue where it might go, how it might grow or what I could build—but it felt like a smart starting point. All I knew for sure was that my content would include tutorials, ideas and techniques on all things DIY. And, I could check off each of my Big 4.

Freedom: I make my own production schedule. Check.

Creativity: I'm designing projects and creating videos, my wheelhouses. Check.

Personal growth: I'm building something completely unique from the ground up. Check.

Relationships: I can work around my family's schedule and needs, plus foster my online community, as well as potentially forge new business relationships. Check.

These reasons on their own made this project perfect for me. However, since I was new to a lot of the techy and strategic side of YouTube, I began researching how to start a successful channel, how to grow subscribers and how to monetize content—all that great stuff. As I learned a ton, I realized the mountain of potential in it.

There's opportunity for passive income and business leads out the wazoo through YouTube. As I watched what other content creators did and how they developed businesses, monetized and scaled through this massive, valuable platform, I began an epic brainstorm and wrote down a slew of ideas. I honestly and carefully assessed all the things I truly believed I could pull off and that I knew in my heart I'd want to do.

Here's what I decided to focus on:

- Write a book
- Develop a presence as a professional speaker
- Create my own course

TIME FOR AN EPIC BRAINSTORM

Now, it's one thing to decide.

It's a totally different thing to act. To actualize as drastic a life shift as I have, you need to do both. One won't—and can't—come without the other. You need to think long and hard about how you want to spend your days, the core of what it is you want in life and how you want your existence to look. But far too often, we do all the thinking and that's where it stops. You can't make a better life for yourself without action. You also can't jump into a new venture without contemplating whether it makes sense or if it's truly right for you.

So, here's my challenge. First, think. I mean, have at it. Ruminate, inspect, consider, ponder, marinate or whatever verb you want to plug in here. Plan some time to have a really good brainstorm about how your version of bliss looks.

Do you love working in the company of others? Does your productivity thrive best while you're working at home or alone? Maybe you need to get your hands dirty. Maybe you find joy working with kids or the elderly. Leading a team might fall into your wheelhouse. The opportunity to travel might check off an important box for you.

Be honest with yourself. Don't settle for ideas that won't serve your ultimate life vision. You deserve that. Come up with a list of actionable ways to implement your version of happiness.

Then, you simply have to go for it.

Maybe your schedule just isn't working, so you need a serious sit-down with your boss to address it, or more dramatically it's time for you to seek a new position. Maybe your path to "happy" is more of a minor shift. Maybe what's missing for you is a new hobby. In that case, you may not need a huge, mapped-out plot to achieve bliss.

Me? I needed a full-blown, explosive life shift that required months of planning to make sure my ducks were comfortably in a row.

But take the necessary time. Have your long, good think about this. Settle on a dream. Then make it a goal and actually map out how you'll do it with proactive preparation.

Then.

Just.

Start.

PART II

GET PAST THE BULLSHIT

5
RISE ABOVE EVERYONE'S PRESSURE

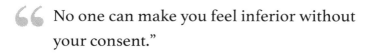 No one can make you feel inferior without your consent."

— Eleanor Roosevelt

You're too sexy, but you're not sexy enough. You're just not as cute pregnant, but when are you going to have another baby? Your hair is way too big. Chop it off, already!

Gang, we're just scratching the surface of my experience with online bullying. Take a look at an actual unprovoked comment I received on Facebook while still working on the Philadelphia morning show (I left it unedited for grammar or spelling):

> "Hey fatso. Enough with the fake laughter already. Jesus Christ, i can see why youre a showbiz reject, and why do you laugh and chuckle when youre talking about bad weather? We're not. We have to travel in it. 80's hair metal wants their hair back. And my god, do you ramble on and on and why does it take you like 10 seconds to swallow? And, why are you so overzealous with the weather as if youre acting. I love when you all are trying to look busy at commercial breaks. Do you get the weather wrong, or does someone else tell you and your just the face?"

Ugh.
That stings.
I know, I know. People's gut reaction whenever I share this kind of hate is always the same, and I'm so grateful and appreciative of the overwhelming support I've received when these comments surface. It always outshines the bad.
"They're just jealous."
"They're totally wrong. You keep rocking it, girl."

"They wish they had your life."

Here's the thing, though. I'm still an ordinary human with pretty sensitive feelings.

One day, I decided to fight back.

A MESSAGE FOR THE HATERS

By June 2015, I was waddling into work like a penguin with cankles.

My feet and ankles had swollen to the size of tree trunks. I was starving all the time. And through my pregnancy—which by a sheer fluke brought us a set of twins—my belly stuck out so much that I was literally off the charts. In case you've never been through a prenatal visit, your ob-gyn will, on several occasions, take a tape measure to your belly to see whether it matches, or falls closely in line with how far along you are in your pregnancy. But with multiples, those guidelines go out the window. In my third trimester, my doctor stopped breaking out the tape measure to track my fundal height, mainly she said, because it didn't quite matter past that point with twins.

Yes, my belly was huge. But I never felt self-conscious about it. Rather, I embraced those 35 weeks when I didn't feel like I had to suck in my gut every time I was on camera. I could just be and it was wonderful.

However, the further along I got in my pregnancy, the meaner the internet trolls became.

"Sticking your pregnant belly out like that is disgusting," someone commented on Facebook.

Then, came the name-calling. "Sausage in casing."

I felt damned no matter what I did. When I wore flared skirts, I was dubbed "old-fashioned." When I wore on-trend, belly-fitting dresses, I was too provocative for a "woman in my condition."

Rudeness became regular commentary on completely unrelated posts about our local weather, and I got so sick of sifting through it. Only after I posted about the seasonal weather pattern El Niño on my Facebook page—provoking another nasty comment—did I finally put my bloated foot down. I'd had enough after this particular nastygram.

I had published my post about the shift in the decadal oscillation and what it could mean for the greater Philadelphia long-term forecast earlier in the morning. Then, I checked out the comments in between cut-ins for the network programming. And there it was: "I don't see why she has to dress like a sausage in casing." It was hard to believe that the commenter didn't think I'd read her words and be hurt by them.

Well, that did it for me.

My hormones weren't in the mood. I marched (well,

sluggishly waddled) the 25 feet from the weather center to my desk and huffily logged into my computer. I typed out a lengthy Facebook post in protest. These assholes weren't just insulting me. They were insulting the unavoidable symptoms and effects of pregnancy. They were targeting women just trying to manage this ridiculously major change their bodies were going through for nine months, while maintaining any semblance of work-life balance. Here's what I wrote:

 A message for the haters...

So, the nature of my job makes me an easy target for criticism. I will always understand that, and I will most typically just ignore it. However, after someone blatantly called me a 'sausage in casing' and another declared that 'sticking your pregnant abdomen out like that is disgusting,' I felt a need to draw a line and speak up.

Everyone's right to their opinion is important, but so are manners. And while rude comments like these will never make me feel the need to change anything about myself, I find a bigger underlying issue here. These particular nastygrams were directed at a pregnant woman.

So this little manifesto of sorts is dedicated to every mother out there—other pregnant moms-to-be, moms reading this while their toddlers play on the swing set, moms whose kids have long since gone off to college...

You are beautiful.

Even during the most uncomfortable—and let's face it, less than glamorous—symptoms of pregnancy, what women go through to bring their precious children into the world is, simply put, AMAZING, and you should be lauded.

Frankly, I don't care how 'terrible' or 'inappropriate' anyone thinks I look. I will gladly gain 50 pounds and suffer sleepless, uncomfortable nights if it means upping my chances to deliver two healthy baby girls. Now it's about more than aesthetics. I want these babies to have the best start possible. And that hopefully means my belly that 'looks like it's about to explode' will continue to grow over the next few weeks.

I say let's raise a Shirley Temple to swollen feet, stretch marks, nausea, all the extra pounds and the dark circles! They're badges of motherhood. And for those of you who think that's 'disgusting,' remember a woman went through the very same thing to bring YOU into the world.

In the meantime, let's all remember the lesson Mom taught us: If you have nothing nice to say, say nothing at all."

I attached a picture of my happy, sun-kissed, heavily pregnant self at 29 weeks standing on the deck of our friend's beach house at the Jersey shore. I read and reread that post five times. Did I have the guts to send it out into the world? I hesitated, stalled some more and then hit post at 10:20 a.m. I told myself, "This message is important. This is basic. This is human and feels vital for me to post."

Then I switched windows in Google Chrome and checked my email, looked at some weather models and checked my phone. As the clock approached 11:30 a.m., it was time to get ready for my final noon show. Before I hoisted my 50-pounds-heavier self up from my desk chair, I logged back into Facebook.

My post scored 1,000 likes and comments in that short hour.

Oh, shit.

If I could insert the little emoji of the guy with the wide eyes, raised eyebrows and mouth rounded into a surprised "oh," this would be the place for it.

My heart fluttered. What had I done? It felt like this might become something far bigger than I intended or expected. By the time I got home, sweating through my maternity dress from the late-August sun, the post had racked up 2,000 likes and comments. I got even more nervous. I thought I was going to get in trouble.

I plodded into the house, plopped my bag on the table, then my pooped self onto the couch. "I think I did something," I said to my husband.

I told him what had happened and the flood of reactions. I pulled up the post, and he read it with a smirk of pride on his face. Ever the supportive spouse, he said, "Hey, it needed to be said."

The next morning, in between shows, our interim news director walked into the weather office and pulled up a chair next to my desk. By this point, the post had in effect gone viral and was racking up thousands and thousands of shares, likes and comments.

Oh, crap. I'm about to get reprimanded. I was ready to get a slap on the wrist. I thought he would make me take the post down.

"I'm really proud of you for that post," he said instead.

I couldn't believe my ears. "We're going to run a story about this and encourage other moms to send in their own bump selfies in support," he said.

IN THE MIDDLE OF 'THE WHIRLWIND'

From that point, through the next week leading up to the girls' birth, it was an actual whirlwind.

I worked every morning leading up to the Tuesday that I went in for an ultrasound—and never left the hospital. But during that span, Yahoo, HuffPost, People, Us Weekly, CBS This Morning, the Today Show, The Doctors, The Ellen Show, Daily Mail, E! News, Fit Pregnancy, Cosmopolitan, New York Daily News and Philadelphia Daily News, plus a few international outlets, all ran stories or made requests for me to comment or appear on their shows.

I received the most supportive letter from the president of Wilmington University with the humbling message that the staff were studying a possible increase in the institution's maternity leave and that my on-air example helped motivate them even more to make that happen. Jaw-dropping stuff.

The most touching moment for me was when Spanx CEO Sara Blakely reached out. She invited me to participate in her coffee table book, "The Belly Art Project." Celebrities and everyday moms-to-be alike had their baby bumps painted with beautiful artwork and then photographed for a collection of empowering imagery.

The timing didn't work out, but a few weeks later, I

received a huge care package full of baby products and Spanx gear. Enclosed—a handwritten note from Sara herself congratulating me on the girls' arrival. I was amazed.

What had happened?

I don't think it had a thing to do with me. Here's what I think happened: I struck a nerve.

One of my favorite moments after "the whirlwind" occurred in my hospital room right after the girls were born. Everything was sore. Even my biggest sweatpants barely fit. I couldn't get out of my bed, stand up or sit down without my husband's help and had yet to recover feeling in all my limbs.

The two of us were alone at the time. Right after she was born, hospital staff whisked Kaeden (my Baby B) off to the NICU. Meanwhile, the nurses were off washing up Parker (my Baby A). Terry, one of the amazing lactation consultants, came in to give me a breastfeeding crash course. Despite sitting through a hospital-sponsored seminar on the subject and reading as much as I could ahead of time, I still had zero clue what to expect or how to approach it.

In full charge of the Bryn Mawr Breastfeeding Mothers Group, Terry was a no-nonsense, get-to-the-point, runs-a-tight-ship kind of gal. Like a drill sergeant in my hospital room, she rattled off need-to-know information about this uncharted territory.

"There are several options to hold your babies during breastfeeding—the football hold, the cradle hold or the lay down," Terry told me, as the details started blending together. "You can use a pillow or blankets to support your babies and get the right position. When it comes to latching, here's how you'll position the babies: Tilt their heads this way, and use this trick to get them to latch on. If they exhibit any of these warning signs, call your pediatrician. You're going to need to pump X amount of times to make sure your supply comes in. Babies need to eat X amount of milk X amount of times per day."

Lord. Help. Me.

Was I in a breastfeeding boot camp? At any second, I thought Terry might scream out, "Drop and give me 20 hand pumps!" She was a wealth of knowledge, but in that moment she was pouring all these staccato breastfeeding bullet points into my one ear, as half of it leaked out the other. She drowned me for a few more minutes while I tried to process as much of her wisdom as possible.

And then, Terry stopped, pausing to take a breath. She dropped her voice a few volume levels and gripped the edge of my hospital bed so she could lean in. With a sweet smile, she said supportively, "We were all so proud of how you handled those jerks on the internet."

It took me a hot second to understand what she had

said. Then I started laughing and gratefully thanked her. Man, that message affected so many people, so many kinds of people.

I received notes and comments from dads-to-be, grandparents, moms in the nearly exact same timetable of pregnancy as my own and about to give birth for the first time, fellow twin moms, nurses, siblings, people half a world away, and women and men from every walk of life, background and upbringing. There was something so relatable in my message: Each of us is here because a woman went through a pregnancy.

Why would we shame that? I don't know. But, man. That keyboard is like an invisibility cloak, removing any filters people might have in their otherwise common-sense brains. I can't say whether the people who've made a point to reach out to me with the sole purpose of being mean and ignorant on social media are actually nice in person, though I'd like to believe it.

Social media, for so long, and still primarily to this day, is a highlight reel. It's a curated version of our existence. It's definitely how I primarily use it, and I still only typically post the good stuff. The prettiest pictures, the most balanced, together version of my family and myself. Most of us don't share our bad or difficult stuff unless we're actively seeking support. After all, the first thing going through my mind after I've just lost it with my twin 3-year-olds isn't, "Gee, I should post a little paragraph describing how I just barked at my daughters and slammed the door so hard a picture frame fell off the wall."

That's not most people's reaction. But an amazing memory as we share the first ice cream cones of the summer at the beach or deck the halls at Christmas? Of course, we all post about those times on social media. Why wouldn't we? We want reminders of our great days. I don't want to be reminded of the time I stepped on the scale and was taken aback at how much I'd let myself go. I don't want to be reminded of the countless times I came home and cried as I relayed my frustrations about work to my husband.

I don't want to be reminded, and I don't want other people to know. That's something that's just been in my DNA as long as I can remember. Over the years, I've so rarely put anything out into the world that would make me look vulnerable. It's how I've protected myself. What no one knows won't cause them to judge me, the choices I've made and the life I lead. I won't have to deal with online hate then, right?

Please.

That protective instinct did squat for me. The nastiest comments I've received on social media were on general posts where the subject matter shouldn't have ignited any vitriol.

On top of it all, a huge and pretty obvious—but still

easy to overlook—lesson I learned through all of this is that I'll never please everybody. There's no such thing as one-size-fits-all except when it comes to those hospital gowns that open in the back. Once I accepted that fact, I felt better equipped to handle the online bullshit with more ease.

THE MANY FACES OF BULLYING

Every time I got attacked online, it felt as though it was coming from the right, left, center and every other direction. However, that negativity was the minority in the grand scheme of the community I was part of online. Over so many years of performing my work in the public eye, I inadvertently built a community of wonderful people: viewers who'd tuned in all throughout my pregnancy to watch my belly grow with double the speed. These faithful viewers kept me in their thoughts, as many of them had gone through the rigors of pregnancy themselves or had a spouse who did.

I needed to remind myself of these people. They were the humans who deserved my attention. Their notes of support meant so much to me. While I was never able to respond to each of them, I read every single message. And to this day, I try hard to keep their good vibes in the forefront of my mind.

Unfortunately, bullying, discrimination, hate and harassment span quite a territory. It's obviously not confined to the web.

Allow me to paint another picture.

Up until the late 2000s, I had no idea how to apply my makeup, style my hair or dress to complement my body type. I always wore an exorbitant amount of dark eyeshadow and the most unflattering lip colors. I didn't know how to apply foundation. I didn't understand the concept of blending. My hair was a constant experiment both in living color and layering. I didn't know what clothing styles I could pull off. My whole look was rough around the edges.

This didn't bode well for a newbie reporter who needed to maintain a professional image on the air. And managers made sure I knew it. They loved to tell me when my outfits weren't working and to give me personal style advice. They made sure I knew when any minute detail of my appearance was out of place.

Over the years, I've been on the receiving end of nitpicking that would shock you. Once, a boss actually licked her hand and swept her spit across my coif to lay flat one flyaway hair. Another time, a manager abruptly pulled me aside in between recordings with life-or-death urgency. "You really need to wear a necklace with your suit," she hissed. "It just completes the look."

Also among the first orders of business when I

began one particular on-air gig: Head to the salon to color my hair. My new boss had the stylist make me a mousy brunette for a few months until I covertly switched back to my original golden blonde. I received multiple text messages over the years, even in the middle of a broadcast, explaining what was wrong with my outfit that day or alerting me that the way my hair fell on one side made it look uneven and shorter than the other side. In my first job after college, I sat in a closed-door meeting to discuss my manager's need for me to invest in more cowl-neck tops.

When I scored my first gig, I was lucky to be making the salary I did in a TV broadcasting job. However, my disposable income was a joke, and the dream of a company clothing allowance was a unicorn prospect. That's why my closet was full of ill-fitting, but affordable, clothes from Joyce Leslie or The Deb. As I built my career, I was paid more and could afford to buy better clothes to make me look more polished. I watched a ton of tutorials to learn makeup techniques. Still, no matter what I did, I could never please everyone. Even after leaving my TV career, I still get negative comments about my hair, my wardrobe, the list goes on. There's nothing easy about dealing with this.

There's also nothing easy about dealing with chauvinistic lack of respect.

#RISEABOVE

While at my broadcasting internship, I helped my friend and mentor Dave with some field production on a pilot. This show was Dave's side project and took an in-depth look at local EMS personnel. Think of it as "Rescue 911" with a local twist.

Cool. It was more experience for me and I was happy to help.

I can't remember the show host's name. It might have been Tom.

But I remember everything else that happened that day.

This show host had a Tom Selleck-as-Magnum-PI vibe going on, but with a late '90s spin. Wavy hair, light eyes, a stache—and decked out in a golf shirt and pleated khakis. That's probably why I remember his name as Tom.

Anyway.

We pulled a full eight hours on a hot Saturday, each of us giving up half our weekend to help Dave. Given the heat, and the shooting location on an asphalt firehouse lot, I dressed casually and as coolly as possible in a white racerback tank top, khaki shorts and sandals. My hair was knotted in a French braid.

One of my main duties? Holding up cue cards for What's-His-Name.

I knelt beneath the camera so the show host could see his script without the obvious tell that he was reading from the cards.

"Hey Katie, can you lift the cards a little higher?" What's-His-Name asked.

"Sure," I replied and raised them up.

"A little higher," he responded. I complied.

"Just a little more." At this point, Mr. Host Man waved his cupped hand in an upward motion, gesturing that the cards need to hang just a *little* bit higher.

I realized the cue card height now revealed my chest.

"Perrrrrfect," he purred.

Dave was mortified. He should've been. Me, I just rolled my eyes in disgust and we carried on.

There were lots of cuts and retakes, and every time, our respectable lead talent made the smarmy hand gesture and sing-songed, "Higher, Katie."

I felt pretty damn demeaned. I give credit to Dave, since he tried to step in and gently request that "Tom" let the fuck up. But it didn't do much good.

Dave checked in with me multiple times. "Is this OK?" he asked, knowing full well it most certainly was not.

When we finished the shoot that day, Dave pulled me aside and apologized profusely for what had happened. I shrugged and said it was OK. And again, we both knew it wasn't.

I didn't expect him to step in on my behalf. Ultimately, it was up to me. However, I'm extremely non-confrontational, so I had no intention of standing up for myself or walking off the set in protest. Whether it was warranted, I'd have felt extreme guilt if Dave's project failed because of how someone treated me. And so, I put up with overt, public sexual harassment rather than put a stop to it.

And that's the story. Yeah, that's where it ends.

It sure doesn't seem like there's a moral here or any justice whatsoever, does it?

Life won't always be fair. We all know that. It's how we move on from the bullshit that defines us. What did I do?

I learned from it.

At the time, I didn't feel enough worth to call out the disgusting treatment or demand an apology. Nowadays however, I know damn well I don't have to put up with that kind of degrading conduct. I'm done letting incidents like that weigh me down.

Example: Once I dated a guy who wanted me to get breast implants because I wasn't shapely enough as my natural self for his tastes. I outright refused his request, although if I'd known I'd look like someone let the air out of my chest after breastfeeding twins for 13 months, I can't say I would've been so adamant back then.

The point? He's an ex for a reason. I dropped that dead weight because I finally recognized my value.

FINDING the humor in these situations can also be incredibly helpful. You can let it get to you or you can laugh it off. As my time on TV wound down, another random nasty remark made it to my comment thread: "katie. you would be so pretty if you combed your hair."

I responded, "I prefer looking like a disheveled troll."

I'll reiterate that I've always been pleasantly surprised by people's positivity and support, which always surpasses the negativity. After I had publicly called out yet another keyboard warrior who told me how horrible my hair looked, my feeds flooded with kind words and encouragement. A gracious man wrote this to me, which I loved: "There's much to love about social media, but it's way too easy [to] hate with the click of a mouse. #RiseAbove"

What a great hashtag: #RiseAbove. (I need to make a #RiseAbove iron-on with my Cricut machine for a sweet T-shirt.) Rise above. It's so fundamental. It's the definition of how I've tried to react to bullying from total strangers on the internet.

Rise above. We should live by those words. We should tell ourselves this in the mirror if that's what it takes. We can be better than this. And we deserve more.

Blocking out the noise is vital to your success and your well-being. You deserve to feel confident. You deserve to be treated well. You deserve decency.

If you're in a relationship of any kind that isn't serving you in these positive ways, handle it. Mute the mofo. Dump his (or her) ass. Kill them with your own kindness. Turn the other cheek.

From what I've learned in my personal journey, there's no one right way to approach this. Different days bring different moods. You'll react differently from moment to moment. My ways of dealing have traditionally been a cocktail of reactions: to mute, block, unfriend, counter, snooze, shrug off, laugh off, or move on quietly and unaffected.

These are all coping methods that I can make peace with after the fact. My suggestion? React in a healthy way that serves and works best for you. (If that means you block their asses, do it.)

My hope is for you to be mentally healthy. Surround yourself with positive vibes. You don't need *their* pressure, so it's time to rise above it.

6
EXPECT NOTHING

> Despite all my rage, I'm still just a rat in a cage."
>
> — Billy Corgan

> Hope isn't a goddamn strategy."
>
> — Jay Scott Smith

From a pretty young age, I had set a high bar. I planned how I wanted my life story to play out. At age 27, I meet Mr. Right. He proposes to me in the most amazing, epic way. We get married in a massive church wedding. In our early 30s, we have a brood of little ones to love and chase after, preferably two boys and a girl.

Where's that guffawing emoji when you need it? What utter hooey. From high school to college into my 20s, I was immersed in the dating game. Mr. Right wasn't raising his hand in the group of less-than-ideal men I met and dated. I knew deep down if I didn't pump the brakes on this life plan I had designed for myself, I'd be highly disappointed—or worse, I'd settle.

My point here? Don't expect anything.

THIS CHAPTER AROSE from a place of anger. See, I suffer from "Care-Too-Much Syndrome," particularly in my work.

Perhaps you can relate.

When you start to feel like the energy you put out doesn't matter, and you feel exceptionally unappreciated or even worse, invisible.

When you make a real effort to work toward providing value—whether it's a service or product—and no one will work with you.

When you actively try to open lines of internal communication and get radio silence back.

When you observe sexuality being valued over experience and aptitude.

These irritating moments of insanity threatened to envelop me whole. After experiencing each of those scenarios to the point of wanting to rip my hair out, I found a way to cope with the frustration: Don't. Expect. Anything.

When you go on a job interview, the hiring manager will often ask what you consider your biggest weakness. The advice I always got from advisors, teachers, or my mom on how to respond to such a question was to say I'm a perfectionist because it was a good problem to have. I get why that sounds good. However, that response rang completely true for me and was, in fact, a weakness.

I've always cared too much. If I had a work deadline, I believed in meeting it. I felt a timely response to colleagues' emails was not just professional, but also polite. I cared obsessively that the information I put out to my viewers was as accurate as possible. I gave a damn whether my work schedule allocated adequate prep time in order that I could present a responsible story to the viewers. It really bothered me when typos made it to the public eye. I cared so much, I was a twitch away from losing my sanity. These issues, which should have been minor and far less frequent, crept up every single day—and it was slowly driving me crazy.

Keep in mind that Care-Too-Much Syndrome differs from hope. Hope's a lovely intangible. The hope that things will change in your favor is something you can daydream about, but if you EXPECT it, you'll find yourself sorely disappointed far more often than you find yourself satisfied.

Don't expect squat. Sounds tough, right? And pessimistically harsh. But think about it. When you don't expect circumstances to work out in your favor, when you don't expect a superior to keep a promise, when you don't expect general outrage when procedures and protocol get ignored continuously, when you don't expect coworkers to give as much of a shit as you, you won't feel so confined. These things can't and shouldn't bind you. Care about the things you can control, since you have the power to change those.

I know I was never alone in my frustrations. I'd come to realize two deeply ingrained truths over my many years in the working world. First, it's still a lot like high school in any company or organization. There are mean girls and the popular people, the insecure set and of course, the gossipers. And second, the same fundamental problems exist for everyone. The only difference is in the details. People feel unappreciated and undervalued, overworked and overwhelmed. Employees have to do more with less. They're still expected to perform quality work despite being ill-equipped for success.

My biggest mistake in trying to cope with this

constant frustration? Letting my discontent start to show at work.

ANOTHER UGLY CRY

"You don't seem happy," I began to hear from viewers on social media, from coworkers and from family. Everyone was starting to notice.

"How's work going?" a friend asked me at his annual Christmas party.

"I hate it," I blurted with a wince, and then promptly took a giant gulp of his fancy spiked holiday punch.

"That's what I thought," he replied knowingly, with no judgment whatsoever. Then, he went back to plating more appetizers.

Dang.

I always knew I wore my heart on my sleeve. Everyone seemed to see right through whatever happy face I put on through clenched teeth. We've already discussed that out of the womb, I was moody as hell. When I'm set up with circumstances and situations that work against me, my emotions amplify tenfold. I still haven't figured out how to turn it off.

One afternoon, I stayed late at the office for a mandatory meeting. Throughout that entire morning, I had slowly developed a fever, headache and began to lose my voice. I knew the best thing I could do was go home and rest. But I had to be there, right? It was a mandatory meeting about our team philosophy and brand messaging. Critical stuff, as far as I was concerned, and incredibly important to the strategy that we as a company had set out to fulfill together.

Even though I was the equivalent of a sorority pledge three chugs of Mad Dog away from passing out from my weak immune system, I didn't peace out on it. I did what any control freak does: I tried to beat the illness at its own game and power through, even though I felt like a fucking Mack truck had hit me. Quite short-sightedly, I decided a quick yoga class at the gym downstairs would do me good. I'd knock out 45 minutes on the mat, then jet back upstairs and hoof it to the opposite end of the building for our important team get-together.

Well, you see where this is going. The stretching and funky positions didn't sit well with me. I remember settling into a crescent lunge twist and thinking I wasn't going to make it through the class, at least not in a state of consciousness. My body wasn't having it even when I attempted to move into the poses I usually nail.

It was a bad call on my part.

I felt so lightheaded that I quite literally drrrrrrrrragged myself back upstairs, actually near fainting on the walk down the hall.

When I finally made it to the opposite side of the building, the meeting was already underway. I was 10 solid minutes late. Rather than interrupting and explaining my tardiness, I sluggishly trudged to an open corner of the table and plopped down, just wanting to put my head down. I clearly wasn't myself.

Oh, and the best part? That super-important discussion we stayed extra hours to have? It got tabled, never to be returned to again (at least while I was an employee of the company).

Are you fucking kidding me?

My very apparent irritation was the proverbial straw that broke the camel's back for my boss.

I was still feeling far less than 100% and had yet to fully recover my voice when he called me into his office a few days later. Whenever I've been asked to stop in to see any boss, I always ask "Open or closed?" and point to the door as I walk through it.

"Closed," he said. Uh oh. He didn't say it angrily, but that's never a good sign.

He started by telling me a story. It was his version of the tale of my disrespectful display in that last meeting.

"What I saw was you walking in late, slamming your stuff down and crashing into your chair," he said.

Worthy of note, that was the first anyone asked what was up with me that day.

"I felt *horrible*, I had a fever," I began to explain in

my still cracking voice, readily diving in to describe how I had felt like literal shit that day. It didn't really seem to matter.

"I'm also hearing from the crew that you're huffy when they ask you to give mic checks," he interrupted.

OK, we're taking a sidestep. The irritable mic check issue. This was probably the second or third time I'd explained this problem to a supervisor and asked for help to fix it. When you feel like you're walking on eggshells with colleagues, having to babysit tasks that directly affect you but aren't your responsibility, getting virtually no communication back, plus just ALWAYS. Being. Tired. It'll take a toll after a while.

I challenge anyone who's never adequately rested, has a front-loaded schedule of deadlines that are all due five minutes ago, and has to stifle the stress on camera before thousands of viewers for nearly three hours to maintain a chipper attitude in perpetuity. Others might hide their frustrations better, but there's exactly zero chance that I'm the only one who'd eventually get noticeably irritable.

We sat for a pregnant pause not making eye contact, me waiting for whatever he'd say next. My boss glanced at the 10 giant monitors showing other TV stations over my shoulder. I could tell he was ready to say something, filtering his words internally before saying them out loud.

"Is something going on that I need to know about?" he asked abruptly. I wasn't emotionally or physically ready for the question. My reaction happened in what felt like slow motion. Even before he finished the sentence, I'd already broken down, bawling. And guys, it was another ugly cry.

This one was far off the charts.

I had a hard time catching my breath. My face flamed red. My nose started running. I was heaving as I attempted to explain my distress. All I could manage to get out initially between sobs was, "I'm (*heave*) just trying to (*heave*) get through."

A sense of horror overcame me. "You MUST stop crying. You MUST stop crying," I screamed on the inside. "Get it together! You CAN'T let him have this impression of you!"

Well, I couldn't stop.

DUMP WHAT'S HOLDING YOU BACK

My last shred of pride was gone. There was no turning back. It was a spiral. I was spiraling.

I had pent up so much frustration, anger, irritation and despair. Like a pre-Katrina New Orleans levee, my emotional gate burst open, leaving me completely powerless to rein any of it in, let alone stop it. My boss sat there, leaning forward, twiddling his pen between his fingers, not quite looking me in the eye, and most definitely not realizing he'd just invited an emotional landmine into his office. He knew I was mortified. And he didn't know what hit him.

After several excruciatingly long minutes, I deep-breathed my way toward gathering some semblance of control. I tried to explain to him why I was feeling so low: I can't get things right with certain colleagues. There's no sense of leadership. I feel like I'm on an island or at least like I'm in the movie "Mean Girls." I'm so uncomfortable that I'm keeping my head down, withdrawing into myself, and just doing my own work. I'm merely trying to reach 12:27 p.m. each weekday.

I know that sounds super self-pitying. It was. But it was truly how I felt.

And on top of the enormous work-related stress I was under, I explained, it had been a particularly difficult week. I was still sick, for one thing.

"Why didn't you say you weren't feeling well when you came late to the meeting?" he asked.

"Because nobody gives a shit!" I shrieked, with way more emotion than appropriate. On top of that, I continued, I'm utterly drained. My voice was shot. One of my little girls had broken her arm. Add that to the already-draining task of rearing twin 2-year-olds.

With that, my boss cut me off and spat out, "Well, I

just put my dog down, but you don't see me crying in my office!"

I was floored. I looked at him, dumbfounded and stunned. All I could say was, "Wow."

My boss quickly wrapped up by backpedaling into saying that the company still valued me and my work. As I headed back to the studio for one final half-hour of TV, I avoided eye contact with anyone I passed in the hall, my red-rimmed eyes looking like I'd just gotten stoned. Right then and there, I decided to never tell my boss anything personal again, until I gave notice that I'd be leaving the company.

While I didn't expect special treatment, I definitely didn't expect my boss's derisive reaction. This encounter taught me once and for all that I'd be best served to not expect anything. I told myself, "Katie, don't expect sympathy. Don't expect compassion. Don't expect pity. Don't expect any help to fix your situation."

Another place to lower your expectations? When common sense comes into play.

Logic incorrectly told me a great chance to grow professionally would be supported by my superiors. I had received an invitation to emcee a huge multi-day event, in front of hundreds of high-level leaders from across the country, including my local market—a really big deal. But it took place during sweeps and in another state, which meant I'd need two days off. When I pitched the value of a gig like this to the big bosses, I was met with, "We only give days off during sweeps for things like weddings or graduations."

"But not when it's a huge opportunity for career development?" I asked.

"Not if it doesn't benefit us."

Oh, OK.

Thankfully for me, something was happening deep in the shadows.

I was blossoming quietly with a new project that was actually serving me. In just six months, I had built a YouTube channel from zero subscribers to 15,000. I was constructing something by and for myself. I didn't know where it would take me, but it was beyond more fulfilling than what I currently received a paycheck to do—a project that fell on my shoulders alone.

I set no expectations of a destination, but was driving this ship—and I was developing really big aspirations. On my mind's back burner, the gears ground slowly, but with powerful force and ambition.

I knew unequivocally that under a corporation's thumb, I'd never achieve any of it. I had to make a choice between the two. And it was a very easy choice in the end.

I had to dump what was holding me back.

NOTHING GETS HANDED TO YOU

So what are the bullshit scenarios going on in your world right now that you can't do anything about?

Here's a better question: What nonsense are you seemingly stuck with that you, in fact, DO have power to change? Assess this. Step outside yourself and really analyze it.

Are you frustrated by and feel like an outsider to the clique-y mom group at the playground? You can change that. Go to another park. Avoidance isn't a bad thing if it's for your mental health.

Are you working with a verbally abusive client and you dread every email or phone call with them? You can resolve that. Talk to your supervisor about the situation and request a change.

Maybe you're trying to eat a healthier diet, but can't seem to stop reaching for the junk. It's hard, but you CAN beat the temptation. Buy your groceries on a full stomach to avoid the snack aisle bait. Kick the garbage food you know you shouldn't eat out of the house. With one good food decision at a time, you can turn your bad binge habit into a healthy one.

But don't expect anything to magically happen for you. I repeat in all caps: DON'T EXPECT ANYTHING TO BE HANDED TO YOU.

Finding your happiness means that you'll work for

it. It means reflection. It means latching onto habits that intrinsically shape your joyful existence. And it means pushback. Find the courage within yourself to call out or reject stupidity, when necessary.

One of my favorite '80s movies is "The Breakfast Club." What a great message for the outcasts of the world. We all have value and purpose. Among the iconic lines is a classic from sexy principal Richard Vernon when he gets some insubordinate lip from mouthy (also sexy) punk John Bender: "Don't mess with the bull, young man. You'll get the horns."

Strong though my affinity to that cinematic gold, I must respectfully disagree, Dick. The metaphor of the bull that represents this world—go ahead and mess with that bull. Take it by the horns and get what you want out of this life. It's yours. You deserve it.

Here's the bottom line, peeps.

You can't expect anyone to fix your life for you. You must do it for yourself. And please, save yourself the frustration if you don't hit a goal quickly or the first time around, or especially if anyone else has a direct impact on whether you succeed or not.

Don't expect your situation to automatically work out. Rather, plan for it.

Anticipate roadblocks and know how you'll sidestep them or react or change course should they arise.

That's how we move forward.

7
EMBRACE THE CLICHE

> Do the best you can until you know better. Then when you know better, do better."
>
> — Maya Angelou

> Don't avoid the cliches. They're cliches because they work!"
>
> — George Lucas

> Every disadvantage has its advantage."
>
> — Johan Cruyff

When the email showed up in my inbox inviting me to present the baccalaureate speech to the 2011 graduating class at my alma mater, Cedar Crest College, I thought they'd made a mistake. I was only seven years removed from earning my degree. How could I find words to inspire, motivate or challenge a room full of brand-new graduates?

Then, I just started typing. I wrote down what had proven to be important advice in my adulting journey so far. Yes, unedited word-processed vomit at first, but the speech turned into something solid. The premise? Cliches—you know, those overused phrases that make our speech or writing "unoriginal"—can actually teach us something.

OK, fine. My speech material wasn't going to launch me into thought leadership. I'll also agree that cliches don't often have a place in original writing. But think about it: If a phrase designed to impart wisdom is overused, doesn't that mean that enough people over time found it helpful or inspiring? Could there be value in some of these cheesy lines that trigger our gag reflexes?

Well, for the purpose of my speech, the answer was hell yeah!

Through a series of personal anecdotes, I told the graduates how cliches helped me achieve success. I regaled them about the time little-preschooler-me carelessly managed to flip my Big Wheel in the middle of the alley next to our first-level apartment.

I ended up with a gash in my nose. It left such a scar that if you catch me at the right angle to this day, you can still see it.

This scar is a reminder to me decades later that "accidents happen," but you can recover, even if it leaves behind a literal or figurative scar.

Your accidents also make you unique.

'REMEMBER YOUR ROOTS'

I gave those new grads a glimpse of my upbringing in a tough, low-income section of town.

I grew up less than a 10-minute drive from the Cedar Crest campus in the center of Allentown, a neighborhood with its challenges. The row home we moved into when I was 7 years old—and where I spent the bulk of my childhood—came with a bullet hole through the living room window.

The walls between these century-old row homes were thin. I inadvertently eavesdropped on countless scary arguments between neighbors over the years. I tried to fall asleep through the raucous sound of kids still roughhousing in the room opposite my bedroom wall at 11:00 p.m.

Our house was robbed twice while I still lived there. The cops made frequent stops at our neighbor's place, sometimes for disturbing the peace, sometimes because someone shot off a gun.

Our neighborhood was a melting pot: Caucasian, Hispanic and African-American, as well as blended families. My brother and I rode bikes and played with all the kids in our back alley constantly.

These were all details of my past that opened my eyes to socioeconomic issues, exposed me to cultural differences, and encouraged me to develop relationships with everybody and anybody in my diverse community.

These and many other stories from my past made me who I am today, so I encouraged that room full of graduates to do as I had done and "remember their roots."

'DON'T SWEAT THE SMALL STUFF'

"Don't sweat the small stuff," I also advised them.

This admittedly has always been a struggle for me, as I bend out of shape over the stupidest, most inconsequential shit.

Here's one of my actual, ridiculous, woe-is-me outbursts: "No! Pier 1 Imports doesn't have the chest of drawers I want in stock! Ughhhhhhh! Now I'll have to wait two weeks to organize my beauty products! My life is over!"

My snowflake tendencies are laughable sometimes, but it's not something I can easily turn off. The first step is knowing I struggle with this, as the old cliche nugget of wisdom advises, "Knowledge is power." The fact that I can recognize this about myself also means I can catch and check myself when I'm taking things too seriously.

This blown-out-of-proportion reaction is usually a byproduct of something bigger going on in my life. So now, I use these ridiculous emotional eruptions as clues to take a bird's view of what's triggering them in the first place.

I look back at the Pier 1 chest of drawers freak-out and know I acted childishly. However, there was a larger underlying issue. This incident happened before I had kids, but I was already beaten down by a schedule I hated. I didn't have an ounce of energy most days for my own projects. So on this one day I motivated myself and found a chunk of quiet, open time. I wanted to knock out the project of reorganizing that little portion of my life: beauty products. It didn't work out the way I planned, so I flipped out.

Now, when I catch myself sweating the small stuff, I step back, look at the overall picture and figure out what's causing this reaction.

'FACE YOUR FEARS'

I recounted how I "faced my fears" on multiple occasions.

OK, don't laugh. Or do, because it's ridiculous.

Here it is: I avoided Starbucks for years. Not because of the expense. Not because I had another coffee shop that was my fave. Not because I didn't like coffee. (Please. Be serious.)

No, I never stepped foot in a Starbucks because I was too afraid to place an order. Dramatic facepalm.

Cut me at least a little slack, if you would.

There's an awful lot of pressure involved for a Starbucks virgin. First, pick what size you want, from options you've never heard of unless you've spent time in Italy. Second, decide what kind of drink you want as a base. Coffee? Macchiato? A latte? From there, your barista needs to know your temperature preference, caffeination choice, milk option, sweetener, shots, flavors and toppings—and the serving size for each.

It reminds me of a scene in one of my favorite '90s movies, "You've Got Mail." Over the then-cutting-edge technology of AOL chat rooms and instant messaging, the characters played by Tom Hanks and Meg Ryan get to know each other, writing emails back and forth like pen pals. In one of these charming email exchanges, NY152 (Hanks' AOL username) describes a version of the internal clam-up I felt any time I considered walking into a Starbucks and just placing a damn order:

> The whole purpose of places like Starbucks is for people with no decision-making ability whatsoever to make six decisions just to buy one cup of coffee. Short...tall...light...dark...caf, decaf, low fat, nonfat etc.... So people who don't know what the hell they're doing or who on Earth they are can, for only $2.95, get not just a cup of coffee, but an absolutely defining sense of self. Tall... decaf... cappuccino!"

Well, it took me a long time to gain my absolutely defining sense of self, but I've long since faced this silly fear. And I started small. Sorry! I started tall.

I marched up to a Starbucks counter one day and ordered a grande caramel macchiato, no fancy alterations. I had no idea what the hell a macchiato was, let alone what it would taste like, but I was willing to spend $4.75 plus tax to find out.

And "the rest is history." My love affair with Starbucks has continued longer than my marriage (as my rewards card anniversary email reminder pointed out to me).

Here's another fear I faced, this time by force. I

learned to navigate the New York City subway system to get to work. Living in New Jersey, 16 miles west of the CBS Broadcast Center, meant driving to work wasn't logical, except for my overnight weekend shifts. The Monday-to-Friday traffic alone made it entirely unfeasible. I also couldn't rationalize the cost of parking after the headache of that commute.

I opted instead for the less expensive, more logistical nightmare of taking a train, then a subway and finally making a multiblock trek on foot. Public transit terrified me because I never used it before. Other than my scheduled bus ride to school for the fourth and fifth grades, I always walked, biked or drove everywhere. But then came my big job in the Big Apple.

The subway scared me more than the train. The train, you see, was above ground, so I could maintain my sense of direction while riding. The subway however, still made me feel that there was a good chance I'd get on a train going in the wrong direction and end up at Washington Square Park instead of Columbus Circle. I explained to the bemused crowd of graduates how confident I felt after tackling that fear of boarding trains in the big city.

Then, I told them about my intense childhood fear of running water.

You heard me.

I was so terrified of running water that once I ran

frantically into our house, crying hysterically for my mother. I wanted her to stop a big, bad slow drip on our outdoor faucet. It's a good thing I overcame that obstacle, since I ended up in the business of chasing storms and reporting from the eyes of hurricanes for more than a decade.

It's a little ridiculous that I told this or any of these stories to a group of graduates. Yet, not all the fears I've overcome were as trivial. Leaving my career was the scariest thing I've ever done. Writing this book came with a ton of self-doubt. My private daydream of opening a DIY workshop would've been such a pivot realistically, nerves nearly consumed me the night I finally brought it up to Steve.

But by meeting these challenges head on and finding ways to confront them, I made things happen for myself that I wanted so badly.

'USE IT TO YOUR ADVANTAGE'

Here's the most meaningful cliche I spoke about to that room of hopeful graduates: "Use it to your advantage."

In many ways, this is obvious.

It makes total sense to use the resources you have at your disposal. For me, that meant burning gallons of midnight oil editing in the Cedar Crest video studio when I was in school. I could snag lengthy windows of continuous study time otherwise unavailable during the day. That meant nabbing discounts with my student ID card. That meant practicing piano for my side gig as an accompanist on the baby grand sitting in a room with killer acoustics at my church because I had permission to use it, plus the benefit of privacy and zero distractions. You better believe I scooped up those opportunities.

But "use it to your advantage" goes far beyond the obvious here.

I'm talking about full-circle meaning. Use "it" to your advantage. "It" can be success or failure. "It" can be missteps along the way. "It" was all of the above for me. Embrace "it" all, because all of "it" has value.

Again, there's some Captain Obvious happening here, but it's worth repeating. It's pretty clear how we can use success to our advantage. You achieve a goal, win an award or earn a promotion. Then, you leverage your win and work your way up to the next level.

I did this with all of my career moves. Later, after I had left TV, I used my newfound energy and time spent not commuting to develop a daily exercise routine, which led me to make better dietary choices, which led me to get in the best shape of my life. Yes, even postpartum.

I did this with my social media strategy on a few levels. I've leveraged authenticity. I won't say I never use filters to make my complexion look less washed out, or that I don't scour my camera roll for the best photo out of 53 selfie attempts. However, I always put the real me out there. People have seen enough fakeness. I don't post made-up anecdotes or inspirational quotes I don't truly love.

Second, I built a presence on social media the right way: 100% organically. No company I worked for ever ran a promotion or a contest to earn me followers. I've never spent one cent on fake followers. While I may not have a six-figure following, each and every one of them are real people. That's not just incredibly humbling, but it's priceless to me and a huge support. That, my friends, is a leverage of success.

Embracing success is the easy part. The flip side is where it gets tough. How do you use missteps and failures to your advantage?

FIX YOUR FAUX PAS

Like many people, I've had a lot of horrible bosses throughout my career.

One hated dealing with his direct reports so much that he automated meetings to physically avoid his employees. Another boss was so scatterbrained and uncommunicative that I figuratively banged my head against the wall trying to get a response to an email.

There was another boss I never heard from, let alone saw in person, unless something needed fixing.

But I had a classic horrible boss at my first job out of college. However, this woman turned out to be one of the best—and worst—things that ever happened to me.

She had hired me, presumably because she saw some potential in me. I scored a meeting with her through a local musical theater company for which I had produced a promotional video as a college project. The members of this nonprofit organization were so happy with what I had done for them that their president called up my future boss to tell her she needed to meet me.

Writing stories for an Emmy award-winning news magazine show made me want to step up and do my best work. My boss clearly loved her role as my mentor. She did teach me a lot: how to write to video, not over video; how to string sound bites and voiceover together into a fluid story; and how to interview the most timid or withdrawn people to elicit more than just a one-word answer. She praised me when I turned in a script that met her approval. But quite often, my work wasn't what she wanted. Oh, and she let me know it, often publicly.

One time I listed what she felt was an incorrect title for someone I had interviewed in a lower third. In case you didn't know, lower thirds are the graphics at the bottom of the screen that tell you the name and title of the person being interviewed in a news story.

"Donator?!?! Who uses the word DONATOR???!!!" she scolded loudly from my 30-square-foot cubicle where my entire department—the director, special projects producer, editors, reporters and photographers—all sat within earshot, pretending not to overhear. "I've never heard that word before!"

She continued her diatribe about how we couldn't use non-words, until that poor grammatical horse was beaten to a bloody pulp on the newsroom floor. By the way, she opted to use the word "donor" as the lower third, though it turns out "donator" is a word with virtually the same meaning.

Immediately following that humiliation, I excused myself to the ladies' room and cried frustrated sobs.

Another time, this boss insisted on voicing my tracks with me in the tiny soundproof booth so she could coach me. Picture this: a low-lit, windowless, soundproofed room the size of a Clark Kent phone booth. I was huddled with someone seemingly hell-bent on finding something wrong. We were so close we couldn't help but rub shoulders.

With every track I voiced into the mic, my boss shook her head at my delivery of the lines and explained—as if to a toddler—that I was doing it wrong. She actually chuckled, as if my little mistakes were just the most adorably amateur things she'd ever witnessed. I felt smaller than I could ever remember feeling, which I should've embraced at the time, considering how tightly squeezed we were in that sardine can of a sound booth.

As the torturous training wore on, she asked me to drop my voice an octave, and then pretend I was reading the line as though I were telling my niece a bedtime story. And in the end, I swear my voiceover sounded exactly the fucking same as the first take I'd done.

Man, it felt like she thrived from picking on me. However gauche her approach, I owe my package writing and storytelling skills to this woman. And it took me a while, but I eventually got over the exasperation and embarrassment. I understood and also successfully applied what she tried to teach me.

Those were missteps, fixable problems and faux pas I could remedy. So I did, and honed my skills.

'IF AT FIRST YOU DON'T SUCCEED...'

There will be times you just outright fail. Crash and burn, lose miserably, wipe out and fail.

My sophomore year in high school, I desperately wanted to be part of the coveted chorale group. These were select singers who got in by rigorous audition only, a process kind of like admissions for top-notch private New York preschools.

But I was smitten like Ariel, wanting to be part of that world. I wanted to be among the posture and poise, the illustrious tone and maturity of this group.

The sweaty palm-inducing audition had me jittery to the point I thought my nerves would devour me. I was terrified of our pompous, balding choir director and his better-than-you attitude. You never wanted to be on his bad side, otherwise he'd publicly ridicule you. (This sure was a theme among my high school teachers, come to think of it.) But even if you sat on his good side, he was a meanie in general as he took pleasure in making fun of others in the presence of anyone.

So it took serious courage for me to sing solo in front of this guy. I sang "Once Upon a Dream" from "Sleeping Beauty" for my audition—a short, light-hearted tune to show off my second soprano range. Then, I sang scales to test my range further. I also performed an exercise in sight-reading to make sure I'd be able to keep up with my peers. I can physically recall my anxiety, my heart beating so hard out of my chest that if you looked closely, you could see my shirt palpitating. My hands were shaky, as was my voice, which I guess served to accentuate my vibrato.

The director eventually heard enough of what I could offer this prestigious choral group, and dismissed me with a fast, "Thank you for auditioning. We'll post the results on the choir room door next Thursday."

As I left, I replayed what had happened and felt I did an OK job. I had adequately warmed up my vocals. I didn't miss a note in the audition. I was on pitch, despite being overrun with nerves.

The week's worth of gut-wrenching anticipation that followed was brutal. Finally, Thursday came around. Heart pounding in my chest, palms sweating again and with cautious optimism, I slowly approached the windowpane on which the list of the 1996 chorale singers was posted.

This was during a six-minute break between periods, so a lot of kids crowded the halls, switching out textbooks from lockers, grabbing gym clothes and quenching their thirst with a quick sip from the water fountain. Other students hovered by the list, so I hung back until I could guarantee a blip of uninterrupted time to learn my fate. As the group thinned, I approached the door. I ran a finger down the typed names, wishing with all my mental might that my name would appear.

It didn't.

I rechecked the list three times, hoping for a magically different result. I hadn't made chorale. I was devastated. The reality settled in as I slowly walked to my next class. When I got home that afternoon, much later than usual because my feet had somehow turned into sad cement blocks on the walk, my mother had already beaten me home from work. While I'd normally talk to her over a snack in the kitchen, instead I dragged myself and my school bag up to my third-floor room. I collapsed onto my bed and bawled my eyes out.

It was a tough rest of the year, as I listened to my choir director make announcements for choralers at the end of normal choir practice. I overheard the group I longed to be part of practicing in the room around the corner from my locker and watched them perform from the wings during the spring concert. It hurt. I was jealous and disappointed. But alongside my sorrow, I spent the rest of 10th grade using this defeat to my advantage.

The disappointment fueled me to perform better when auditions came around again the next year. I practiced my sight-reading more. I tried to be a model choir member, showing up for every practice on time and exuding genuine interest. I purposely sat next to a chorale second soprano upperclassman to observe and learn from her—how she worked during rehearsal, the notes she took, and her posture, work ethic and maturity. I took it all in, learning her methods and applying them to my own, with the fervent hope of making the cut my junior year.

The next year, I auditioned for the second time. And this time, I made the Allen Chorale.

What's that cliche? "If at first you don't succeed, try, try again." That 1,000% applies here.

EMBRACE 'IT' ALL

Failure is liberation. But it's an incredibly hard lesson to apply and tread through.

Realize though, once you've failed, you can only get better. Once you've hit bottom, there's only one way to go. Up.

If you can dust yourself off and try again, Aaliyah-style, you've created personal resolve and strength that no one can touch. And the next time you're bumming over a failure, ask yourself this question: Will this failure matter five years from now?

If the answer is yes, spend reasonable time with it. Grieve, settle with your feelings and then slowly heal. But if you can honestly say whatever's happened to put you in such a sorry state won't matter five years from now, I want you to spend just five minutes on it.

Set a timer. Seriously. Set a timer on your phone for five minutes. You can use those five minutes as you see fit. Cry, get angry, scream or blush. But once that alarm goes off, after those few minutes have elapsed, forget it. Shrug off this failure figuratively and literally. Tell yourself you're done with it. The mental and physical action of letting it go can work wonders.

There's another facet to failure that I'm a firm believer in, and it's this: You have to get knocked down and humbled at least once in your life so you can rise higher than the rest.

You need to appreciate losing. You need to get pushed through the grinder. You need to be struck down from a high horse. Didn't get into your dream school? Learn from it. Didn't land that amazing job opportunity? Embrace what that failure can teach you as you approach the next job interview. Screwing up and failing has made me smarter and far more self-aware.

So, use this stuff. Use it to your advantage. Use everything as a lesson or reason to be stronger next time. And if you go down the wrong path, it's never too late to backtrack. But don't leave lessons you've learned on the trail behind you. Use them.

How else do you think I can say I have nearly zero regrets?

I spent well over a decade in broadcasting. I've honed my skills in on-air presence, ad-libbing, production, reporting, videography, editing and writing.

And then I left the TV business.

Trust me, the last person this irony gets lost on is

me. But here's the thing: I don't view any of this experience or time as wasted.

That wealth of experience set me up to use my unique skill set in a way that made me passionate for my work. I also can't even wrap my head around all the other things that would never have happened in my life had I not taken this path. We could go down a serious butterfly-effect rabbit hole here. Had I not gone to school for communications, I'd never have gotten the job reporting and working under that difficult boss who taught me almost everything I know about quality package writing.

That would never have set me up to get hired at AccuWeather, where I met the love of my life, and in the town where I met the best group of friends I've ever known. Therefore, I'd also never have received the chance to level up in market number one.

Think about it. Everything we do, thrive at and fail through can assist us as we make future choices. Embrace it all. The success, the missteps and the failure.

ENJOY THE JOURNEY

Let me tie a bow on this chapter with just one more cliche, which is a quote John Lennon made famous in "Beautiful Boy": "Life is what happens to you while you're busy making other plans." One of the biggest lessons hitting bottom taught me was that you need to love what you're doing every day.

If all you're doing is working hard for an end game of retirement or financial gain, you're not living your life with joy. You're working toward a life you think will bring you joy. Big difference.

I was done trying to get through each day. I wanted to love Mondays and every other day of the week. One of my favorite motivational influencers is Gary Vaynerchuk, and one of the most important lessons he reinforces is the importance of loving your process. In other words, don't work at something you don't love. If you're trying to move up the corporate ladder because you want a high-paying job, yet you hate the corporate life, you're doing it wrong. The hope is that you're loving the everyday tasks that will eventually get you to your end goal.

Strange as it sounds, I prefer setting up a makeshift office space in a coffee shop to stepping into an editorial meeting with a killer view of the Philadelphia skyline. I'd rather hole up in my half-finished basement studio cave to record a video than report to an HDTV studio every day.

What you're supposed to want doesn't need to match up to what will actually bring you bliss.

Remember that. Only you know what truly lights that fire in you.

But remember this, too. Your life is happening right now. Are you spending too much time just getting through, working for the day when you'll finally be able to relax or enjoy more time with your family?

Do an important solid for yourself and look at how you spend your days. Do the bad days outnumber the good? Are you just trying to get through each day? Do you love your process?

Only you can answer this truthfully. Your honest answer is a huge first step to finding your happy place. Life is indeed what happens to you when you're busy making other plans. Consider that now may be the time to change the plan and create a life you can live with joy each day.

That said, not everything I've learned over the years boils down to a catchy cliche. A good portion of the fundamentals I try to live by are simple truths, and I'd like to share those with you, too.

8
BEAT THE CRAP OUT OF INTERNAL BATTLES

> If there is no struggle, there is no progress."
>
> — FREDERICK DOUGLASS

I'm not a violent person. In fact, I'm a chicken when it comes to physical confrontation.

One afternoon in sixth grade, I was minding my own business as I walked the eight blocks home from school. I had taken a different path than usual that day. Typically, I walked Washington Street down to 8th. I felt like a change of scenery that day, so I hoofed the extra block over to walk parallel to my normal route, working my way down Green Street.

As I walked down the tree- and row home-lined residential path, a group of four or five girls started to catch up to me. One girl singled me out. As she and her crew came up on bespectacled me and my purple JanSport backpack, she spit in my hair. Her girls just laughed. I stopped and cowered there stupidly watching as they cracked themselves up over pathetic me. They continued on their way. Fearfully, I didn't say one word.

But I did tell my mother when I got home. She was so angry that she called the school and forced a meeting with the principal to handle the situation. Terrified, I begged her to not make me go through with this. She wouldn't back down and I know she was right. But in my 13-year-old head, I didn't want my bully to "get taught a lesson." I thought my wimpy butt would end up getting bullied far worse in retaliation. This girl was at least a foot taller than me, and heads above me in the scrappy-and-tough department. Luckily, she never tried to get revenge.

OK, so we've established I'm a wuss—at least I was.

However, I've built strength on other foundations. I've fought some intense battles in the last few years.

These battles have two things in common. One, they're internal and self-imposed. And two, no one else could point them out to me.

I had to understand these fights for myself.

STOP TRYING TO BE PERFECT

I've never achieved perfection, but not for want of trying.

When I was in third grade, I got accepted into the gifted program. So during fourth and fifth grades, a small group of us bussed from our low-income section of Allentown to another elementary school in the West End, a far more affluent part of town. From a scholarly standpoint, it was a great opportunity. But from the socioeconomic side, the situation produced a whole lot of unintended consequences.

As a kid commuting into a neighborhood I didn't live in, I felt like an outsider, even an intruder. But I made friends. My squad was pretty small, and we had a blast. We were a mixed group made up of West Enders and center city dwellers who made the commute for the gifted program.

We practiced lip-synced routines for the school talent show at recess. We hung out at each other's houses all the time, where we'd play Barbies for hours. When we took a break to snack on Herr's potato chips and iced teas, we'd sprawl around our bedrooms, and leaf through "Seventeen" magazine, stopping to swoon over pics of Christian Slater, Keanu Reeves and Vanilla Ice. We'd test each other with the revealing questions in that month's quiz: "Are You Stressed?" "Are You a

Fashion Whiz?" "Are You Paranoid?" We'd take turns hosting sleepovers, where we'd tell ghost stories, watch New Kids on the Block music videos on VHS repeat and prank call boys we liked.

One day, my best friend in the group shared something that crushed our innocent fun. She, like me, took the bus across town. She overheard the mother of one of our tightly knit circle call us "street kids." That cast a self-conscious shadow over us, hanging over every social gathering from that point forward.

In high school, all the kids from every neighborhood headed to the same school. William Allen High School was incredibly diverse, with a broad mix of races, ethnicities, income levels and social statuses. I mingled with kids from the West End and every other direction. Much like in elementary school, the kids all hung out at each other's houses after school and on weekends.

When I invited one of my new friends over to my house, he told me his mother wouldn't let him because I lived in a "bad neighborhood."

I felt inferior.

For reasons like this, I started only showing the parts of my life and personality that I thought others would accept.

My first serious boyfriend introduced me to some pretty cool musicians. I loved Duncan Sheik. The original Matchbox Twenty album was pretty damn good, too. One day, he popped in the debut CD of this new artist, Patti Rothberg. Her sweet, slightly raspy voice and rocker chick vibe mesmerized and drew me in.

She had a song called "Perfect Stranger" on this album, and while it wasn't her hit single, it spoke to me. The song is about this guy she sees across the room. She doesn't know him, but she's sure just by looking at him that he's perfect. He's an outline and she fills in the rest of who he must be, creating this immaculate guy in her mind.

> *I built you up in little clay constructions in*
>   *my head*
> *And I like what I see...*
> *What I think you are is all I see*
> *And as long as you're a stranger,*
> *You'll stay perfect to me...*

I could recreate *that*, my subconscious told me. Me, as an outline to other people, letting them fill in what they believe about me. No one needs to know where I grew up. No one needs to know I never talk to my father. I don't even know where he lives. No one needs to know I wear my Express button-down blouse to school every week because it's the nicest shirt I own and

I'm trying to fit with the in-crowd. No one needs to know we ration milk at home because it needs to last until Mom gets paid again and can buy groceries.

The past hurt I'd experienced often led me to pretend I was something I wasn't. I dated guys I wasn't actually into because they came from "better" families, were athletes, or were physically attractive but had nothing in common with me. I applied for a job at Abercrombie & Fitch because I thought I'd look cool if I worked there. I weaseled my way into parties and social circles to count myself among the popular crowd. I was a walking teen '80s movie, straight out of "Can't Buy Me Love" and "Teen Witch," never imagining I'd be accepted by being myself.

It's easier to see how that spiraled so far out of control in recent years, isn't it?

Perfection is unattainable. Everyone has a different definition of it and everyone has flaws. Letting go of imperfections so we can "just be" is crucial to our personal happiness.

JUST START ALREADY

Procrastination. I have long struggled with putting things off, making it my biggest productivity shortfall.

When I had lengthy papers to write in school, I'd look at my semester calendar and think, "Whew, this is a big assignment. Good thing I have months to knock out this 25-page monstrosity before the deadline. I'll just chill for a few weeks."

Then, as the deadline crept up, I'd half-ass my way through the assignment, knowing it wasn't my best. I'd always kick myself for not starting sooner.

Without a doubt, I procrastinate because I worry a project will be too difficult to complete. My easy fix to this: Set a specific goal, list out the tasks to achieve it, and earmark actual time to knock out the work.

When I was still working the early schedule on TV, I consciously used my break to work on my YouTube channel, building graphics and editing. I had a finite amount of quiet time without toddler or colleague interruptions five days a week to knock out these tasks. I got more done in the short hour of break time than I could in the six hours I had at home before I went to bed. The work itself isn't actually hard. It's our mindset or our approach that makes it seem harder.

Here's my disclaimer. I'm not saying that some things aren't hard. Pull-ups are hard. Geometry proofs are complicated. However, there's a whole lot that's not hard. It's just tedious. As a first-time parent, caring for twin infants wasn't hard. It's tedious and tiring. Changing more than a dozen diapers a day wasn't hard. It's tedious and stinky. Feeding twin infants just means you won't have a spare hand to do anything else until they're done eating. It's not difficult to wash two babies' accumulation of dirty bottles and nipples, not to mention entire loads of laundry on a daily basis. It's tedious, and requires an ample supply of moisturizer to avoid dishpan hands.

Differentiate what's actually challenging and what you may be finding excuses to put off. Let's say you want to reach your goal weight. While getting there is a challenge, if you break down your end game down into monthly, weekly and daily goals, you can attack it with a winning mindset. Every day, as you complete your goals, check them off and call it a victory.

What if your dream is to open a small business? Tall task, sure, but it's most certainly not unattainable. You start by seeking out the resources to learn about accounting, leasing a space, budgeting, running daily operations, hiring, managing your operation and so on. I 100% agree that diving into unknown territory is daunting. But when you can approach it with an "I can do this" attitude and a one-day-at-a-time mentality, I guarantee the venture won't seem as scary.

And writing this book? I never thought I had it in me to be an author. Yet, here I am. First, I lined my wall with Post-it Notes to gather my thoughts. I mind-dumped ideas into a Google Doc, which expanded into several Docs and then into several sections of Docs.

I stuck with it, setting at least three hours aside to

write several days a week. I set an initial goal of 40,000 words. I knocked out at least 2,500 coherent words per week. The process wasn't easy, and I grappled with self-doubt. But I kept writing.

You. Will. Hit. Roadblocks. With. Anything. Difficult.

Please keep pushing.

Here's my point, gang. You can do it. Stop telling yourself it's too hard.

We need to rephrase here. If your dream is worth working for, then you'll have to work. The process may not be simple. And it's OK to think the process is hard.

You'll need to invest time and effort into what may prove challenging or tedious, but remind yourself of the end goal.

Don't fall victim to the word "too." Because it's not "too" hard.

You CAN do it. But you're going to work for it.

DON'T ASSUME YOU'RE UNWORTHY

I developed some definite habits while working as a meteorologist for a local morning show.

I always had a travel mug of piping hot coffee at the ready as I put on a full face of HD makeup. I always had an audiobook or playlist cued up as I prepped. When I walked into the office at 3:30 a.m., it was religiously business on top and work from home meets the walk of shame on the bottom. I always wore sweatpants under my dress, since it was meatlocker freezing in the studio that early in the morning.

I always carried two sets of shoes. I'd wear flats or sandals into the office and during most of the show. This was a move I made primarily for comfort, but also for my own personal safety. It was entirely too easy for an already clumsy person who's chronically exhausted to accidentally slip on the slick painted floor or trip over camera cables scattered all over the place. The other shoes I always brought were a pair of heels necessary for attending important meetings, greeting in-studio guests or posing for the one full body shot of the entire morning team at the end of each show.

However, some of my ingrained habits undermined me. I always checked out what my competition was saying. It's smart to see how other meteorologists handle upcoming weather events, particularly to make sure you're accounting for all variables. But I did it because I distrusted my own ability, especially since I'd just rolled out of bed an hour earlier. I'd second-guess myself any time my take on a tricky, or even basic forecast didn't match up to my competitors' solutions.

Predicting the future is an inexact science and Mother Nature is a wild card. Forecasters along with any type of analyst—sports, political, financial and so on—obviously do get it wrong sometimes. But without fail, I tweaked my own forecast to fall more in line with what everyone else said. I didn't trust my own knowledge and gut instinct about the Philadelphia weather pattern, and I'd often kick myself over it.

This happened countless times.

I'd expect fog to develop before sunrise. When no other meteorologists included fog in their forecasts, I'd drop it from mine assuming I must be overthinking it. Then, sure enough, low clouds formed in the countryside.

I'd think I should lower the high temperature on our Jersey shore weather graphic because an onshore wind developed and I wasn't sold the clouds would break enough to warm the coast that much. But if no other forecaster allowed for tough-to-break cloud cover, I'd delete my prediction and accept I must have it wrong. You guessed it. The clouds never broke.

I'd see scenarios coming. But instead of boldly making less popular predictions, I chickened out and followed the herd.

So here's the lesson: This is a confidence issue. Muster the courage to trust yourself and your gut. Don't succumb to what everyone else says or believes if it doesn't fall in line with your own thinking. Someone's fancy title, prestige or pile of awards doesn't automatically trump your perspective.

Of course, there's a balance here. Taking guidance and advice from someone who's been there and has authority on the subject makes total sense. I'd wholeheartedly trust Ellen DeGeneres to weigh in on whether a particular joke would land with the crowd in my first standup routine. Unquestionably, I'd accept coaching from Ali Krieger on how to defend on a soccer pitch. I'd listen intently to (and drool over) Rachael Ray's method for cooking a perfect panini.

Listen judiciously to others, but don't just assume they know more than you. You, my friend, have value in the discussion. Trust yourself.

SURROUND YOURSELF WITH THE RIGHT SQUAD

It's absolutely crucial to surround yourself with people who inspire, motivate, value and *love* you. For me, the most concentrated group of those people lives in State College, PA, home to the Penn State Nittany Lions and a small town atmosphere I embraced. My husband once described living there this way, "It's like you're in a bubble."

Aside from how easy it is to check off annoying, but necessary, tasks like renewing your driver's license or getting an oil change, State College is nicknamed Happy Valley for a reason.

The Penn State community is connected, dynamic and lots of fun. Surrounded by farms and mountains, the town's quaint and manageable, with ample bike paths lining the neighborhoods.

I loved living there. What I cherished more than anything by far was the coolest group of people I'm lucky to call friends—from Queen and Heart karaoke battles royale to "Dancing With the Stars" and "Anchorman" watch parties, from epic backyard cookouts complete with New Jersey and Pittsburgh accent impressions to pub crawls in honor of Ernest Hemingway's birthday every July. I can let loose, be 100% myself, laugh till my belly hurts and get total acceptance from this gang.

We need people like this for so many reasons. A support system of people you can trust, laugh with and count on is priceless for your happiness. It's particularly important if, like me, you tend to absorb a room's vibe. If the tone is uncomfortable, awkward, irritable, angry or frustrated, I take on that bad energy, which makes me feel like crap. That's when I turn to my squad.

Obstacles will still crop up in life.

If you arm yourself with a badass army of compadres, it's easier to move past them, with your sanity intact.

KNOW WHEN IT'S TIME TO WALK AWAY

I spent a lot of years at a job where I was repeatedly ignored, passed over or treated differently. I finally stopped caring—until I finally left the company.

Here's how it played out for me: I got thrown in the deep end of the pool from the second I walked in the door. I could only keep my head above water from that moment until the day I left. I never felt as though I fit in, partly because even before I walked in the door each day, I was already dangerously close to missing my first task deadline. There was almost never time for small talk or getting to know coworkers. The general vibe I got from colleagues was how "shitty a workplace it was." (That didn't start me off on a very hopeful note.)

From day one, I had no formal workplace orientation or onboarding. I didn't know my way around the entire building for years, partly because I never had a proper tour. Despite my repeated requests, it took almost three years to get my business cards. I never went through a performance review, so got very little feedback or any opportunity to develop goals to work toward and better myself.

Getting one-on-one time with a supervisor to discuss critical workplace issues was near impossible (I had three different bosses in three years). Repeated appeals for a schedule restructure to maximize workflow and efficiency went ignored. The resources kept diminishing, but the assignment list kept growing. Different employees enjoyed different standards and I actively witnessed preferential treatment.

I coped by putting on blinders in the office and focusing solely on my own work, not offering more than what it took to get my paycheck every two weeks. The discontent finally became too much. I hit my last proverbial wall and knew it was time to walk away.

The day my superiors called a meeting to discuss my future with the company, I walked into that office with a prepared speech and confident resolve. (Damned if I was going to allow my emotions to get caught off guard again.) I calmly told them I would not be renewing my contract, and explained that I could no longer work with my current situation or expect anyone to fix it for me.

This isn't called quitting.

This is being realistic.

Even if you feel trapped, you don't need to settle for a toxic workplace situation. You don't need to allow an abusive relationship to continue, even if you've invested loads of time and energy.

You have the power to leave. Know when it's time.

PURGE THE NEGATIVITY

Entrepreneur and motivational speaker Jim Rohn said, "You are the average of the five people you spend the most time with."

That's why you deserve to be around and uplifted by people who bring you joy, help make you your best person, encourage you, build your self-esteem and optimism, and influence you to make positive decisions.

It's time to purge the negativity.

Be like Elsa in "Frozen" and just let it go.

Unfollow, unfriend, unsubscribe, and just quit the messaging, situations and people that leave you frustrated. If someone's social posts routinely upset you, you don't need to purposely have that showing up in your feed. Unfollow that account.

If you've been holding onto a friendship that drives you crazy, bail on it. Seriously. Even if it's your best friend since kindergarten, people change, girl! Parting ways with someone you've grown apart from isn't tragic. Sometimes it's best to accept your differences and move on without each other.

There's a flip side to this. Life coach Tony Gaskins said, "You attract what you are." Ask yourself honestly, do you embody the traits you'd want in a best friend, a mentor or a partner? While we need to weed out what doesn't serve us, we also must embody the traits we expect and seek in others.

So much of what we need to work on can never begin unless we know it's a problem in the first place.

My challenge to you: Work on recognizing your weaknesses. Then, take steps to strengthen yourself.

PART III

LET'S DO THIS

9
FEARLESSLY BE YOURSELF

> Cause I'm fearless, nothing that can break me. Hero of my story, I'm a warrior."
>
> — Kellie Loder

> All your kids want is you—not every other Mom you think you should be. All they want is you, so be the happiest YOU there was."
>
> — @CatandNat

The premise of this chapter comes in the form of a challenge, especially if you have years of bad habits to undo like me.

Being fearless is terrifying. How's that for an oxymoron? Think about it, though. At the root of being fearless is being yourself. The real you.

And that can be scary.

I promise, the real you is so much more appealing than anything fake. If that means pulling out a cross-stitch project on an airplane, so be it. If that means rocking an "old man" sweater when your office is freezing, do it. Always do you.

Claiming carefree abandon of anyone's expectations, or what you think anyone wants you to be is one of the biggest steps you can take toward leading your happiest life possible.

Here are some lessons I've learned about being myself.

GET OVER YOUR EMBARRASSMENT

In the shower, my 10-year-old self cheerfully sang, "Going to the chapel, and we're gonna get married..."

I was in my own steamy karaoke zone, shoulders shrugged and fingers snapping. Ten minutes later, as I headed toward my bedroom wrapped in my towel, my mother passed me in the hall and laughingly said, "Well hello, Miss Opera Singer!"

My face turned beet red from the embarrassment of being caught when I thought no one was listening.

Music was always my thing as a kid. I loved singing and playing the piano, and wanted to be part of any choir as far back as my memory goes. I sang in the children's choir. Then, the youth choir. Then, youth choir *and* adult choir. In middle school, I sang in the regular chorus and then the pop ensemble.

Even though I was at my most awkward stage, with Coke bottle glasses, an untamed head of hair, and zero fashion sense, performing with the pop ensemble made me feel euphoric. In seventh grade, our director booked us for a record number of gigs during the Christmas season. With every repetitive show at a nursing home, holiday festival or concert, I developed a love of being on stage, learned to deal with the immense nervousness and believe in myself.

In high school, I participated in every single musical group, and got accepted to the special music-intensive program that launched when I was a junior. Yet, despite the many years of singing in every school choral group, solos at school concerts, singing "O Holy Night" at candlelight Christmas Eve church services, an unsuccessful attempt to audition for "American Idol," and even a brief stint in college majoring in vocal performance, I'm still embarrassed to sing in my true voice in public on a whim.

Wait a second. Hold the phone.

As I recollect this story now, my attempt to get on "American Idol" was hilarious, but I went unabashedly into the challenge as *myself*. My friend Hillary and I made the 90-minute trek east on I-78, splitting toll expenses and blasting the radio. We crashed on the floor of an old friend's hole-in-the-wall studio apartment in Bayonne, NJ the night before to avoid some of the traffic the next morning. We should have spent the night on the sidewalk in front of the audition venue. The line wrapped so far around that New York City block, there was no prayer of us getting in to audition. (This was one of the early seasons when the room could be particularly harsh since Simon Cowell was still a judge.)

I wore an ivory satin corset top, chocolate brown flare dress pants and wedge-heeled loafers. My hair was even worse. Do you remember Christina Aguilera's music video for "Come on Over"? She sported professionally colored, meticulously spaced cherry red streaks through her platinum mane. I attempted the same look hoping to make an amazing first impression on Simon. I bought a cheap hair-coloring kit at CVS to turn only a few sections of my blonde tresses into this hip, bright red shade.

Surely, this would help me stand out.

As I brushed the maroon goop into my hair, it didn't look like I had applied enough to my wet head. The color didn't pop. Rather than read the clear instructions explaining that's how it was supposed to look, I decided I should run streaks through my entire head of hair. What a disaster: Two-thirds of my hair, once rinsed and dried, looked like the Kool-Aid Man attacked me. Since I never made it through the "American Idol" audition door, let alone on national TV, I assume there was divine intervention at work.

Think about that for a second. I gladly would have gone on national TV in front of millions of viewers with my hair color trainwreck. But I always refused to sing in public and lacked the self-assurance to do so unless it was an official performance or karaoke night, unless it was requested of me or I was given permission.

But wait. There's more.

I have another dark, dirty, guilty pleasure.

I love embroidery.

It's another hobby I fell in love with as a child. My mom has quilted, cross-stitched, needle-worked, crocheted, knitted and sewn her way through life. She'd rarely show up to a family function without her tote bag of yarn and needles—and she made no apologies for it.

My interest in it piqued after watching her turn a skein of yarn into a gorgeous crocheted baby blanket.

She stitched a few folded pieces of gold fabric into a magical hand-sewn Belle costume, which I wore when I sang "Beauty and the Beast" for my middle school spring concert.

Mom taught me all her skills: I know how to knit one, purl two. I know how to thread a sewing machine. I know how to crochet my own afghan. Of all my stitching skills, my favorite is cross-stitching. The complexity of these works of art amazes me. You can actually stitch a Thomas Kinkade painting onto canvas. For real, this craft takes time and intense attention.

For years, I've been working on a Christmas-themed project. It's a super-intricate, 8-inch-by-10-inch pattern of Santa peeking out a window as he's about to hang a candy cane on the Christmas tree. There's a ton of detail, with fresh snow glistening on the window sill and a wooden sled leaning against the wall. There are four different shades of dark green for the tree branches and eight different shades of red for Santa's suit. And the plethora of whites: eggshell white, off-white, ivory white, true white and so on. Before I had kids, I spent quiet weekends watching Netflix movies, keeping my hands busy with cross-stitch.

Etsy upped my hobby's cool factor, offering patterns with more millennial and humorous themes to modernize an outdated "grandmas-only" craft. I eagerly browsed the online shops one day. My eyes twinkled with excitement at the treasure trove of hip cross-stitch designs, quoting "Arrested Development" ("There's always money in the banana stand"), "The Office" ("That's what she said") and even DMX lyrics ("Y'all gonna make me lose my mind, up in here, up in here").

I bought three kits: a small cartoon portrait of the best foursome ever to grace the small screen: Dorothy, Blanche, Rose and Sophia in "The Golden Girls." A large 16-inch-by-20-inch design of the "Dayman" lyrics from "It's Always Sunny in Philadelphia."

And the real gem, a little five-word quote in an old-fashioned script font with a floral and vine border, framed off in a small embroidery hoop. At quick glance, this piece looks as though I swept it up at an Amish gift shop in Lancaster County. Look closely. It reads, "I am a fucking heirloom."

For the longest time, I was thoroughly embarrassed to pull out my craft in public, or around any guy I dated and even around friends. On more than a few occasions, I boarded a plane in preparation for a long flight with my little project tote bag in tow—canvas, embroidery hoop, extra needles, TSA-approved scissors and pattern at the ready. Then, I'd decide not to take out my cross-stitch work because I was afraid the person sitting next to me would think I'm lame. I'd let my self-consciousness get the better of me, and I'd pull out a book instead.

Clearly, I have a selective embarrassment problem. I'll jumble my words on live TV or share my bloopers on social media. But bust out an embroidery project on an airplane? No friggin' way.

How do I get over the embarrassment? By actively facing these silly insecurities.

A "How to Cross-Stitch" video is in the works for my Katie Fehlinger DIY YouTube channel, which will brazenly declare that cross-stitching is cool.

And, that singing thing? I mindfully sing with my daughters in my real voice. We sing the "Paw Patrol" theme song and all the Christmas carols.

For me, these are realistic, attainable actions toward confidence. Whatever our embarrassments, we can baby-step our way out of them.

JUST TRY IT

Sixth grade gym class introduced me to field hockey, which I loved. Trexler Bulldogs, represent!

While I don't typically characterize myself as being very good at sports involving a ball, I was decent at field hockey. My hand-eye coordination actually kicked in when I needed to connect my stick to the ball. The nearly daily ritual of riding my bike 29 blocks to my grandparents' house to go swimming the previous summer gave me the endurance and strength to keep up for two game halves of 35 minutes apiece. Unlike in other phys ed sports, I never got a nervous pit in my stomach when my gym teacher put me in to play.

However, I never tried out for the team because I automatically pegged myself as unathletic. Two of my aunts played and coached softball when they were younger, but other than them, I didn't grow up in a sports-playing family. This is one of those rare exceptions where I regret a choice I made. I regret the team friendships and memories I didn't make, and the confidence I didn't gain. That's tough to swallow.

I'm passing that lesson learned onto my daughters.

As they're getting older, their personalities are shining through and they've begun expressing healthy fear. Parker absolutely loves swing sets. She delights in going as high as she can on the swings, squealing as we push her, "Higher, Mommy! Higher, Daddy!"

Of course, she'd naturally love the swing ride at the amusement park, right? You know the one: It's the giant tilted carousel of airborne swing chairs that goes around moderately fast. Parker was finally tall enough to go on this "big kid ride" at Sesame Place. We got in line three separate times. She psyched herself up, saying, "OK, Mommy, I'll be brave and go on the swing ride *this time*," in her matter-of-fact, high-pitched voice.

Each time we got in line, even when we worked our

way right up to the gate, she decided she wasn't ready. That was OK with me.

As we drove home later that afternoon, we discussed her fear. "Honey, why didn't you want to ride the swings?" I asked, glancing back at her in the mirror.

"Well, I was scared," she explained calmly from her car seat.

"Sometimes we're afraid of things and that's OK," I told her. "It's good to be afraid, because some things might be dangerous or unsafe. But Parker, sometimes there are things you don't have to be afraid of, like the swing ride! I know you were nervous, but I think it's something that if you tried, you'd really love! Sometimes there will be things I'll ask you to try, because I believe you'll love them. Do you understand?"

"Yeah," she replied with a thoughtful expression, then went back to watching the turnpike scenery that lulled her into a nap.

I was proud of how I explained fear to Parker, who recently told me, "Mama, I think I can be brave the next time we go to the swing ride."

"That's great, Parker!" I said excitedly.

That felt like progress.

I may have missed my opportunity for middle school field hockey, but I'll do my best to encourage my daughters to courageously try new things.

The option of joining an adult kickball league or

something fun like that has also set up a cozy corner in the back of my mind.

SHOW YOUR BEAUTIFUL SELF

For a long time, I refused to mention my age.

I didn't want to face any stigma that still came with it for women. I didn't draw attention to my birthday on July 1. I didn't even put my birthdate on my social media accounts.

Wisdom definitely comes with age, and frankly, as I was close to turning 40, I felt better in my own skin than I ever had. On my 39th birthday in 2019, I posted my age on social media. I also posted a completely natural photo of myself. No makeup, still in sweats having just gotten out of bed:

 This is 39.

> I know a lot of you are used to waking up to the (mostly) polished, done version. But this is the real me. Hair unwashed, post-allergy attack eye bags (how am I still having them in July?!) and those damn dark circles.
>
> But I'm sitting on my deck, listening to the birds with a cup of coffee, and I'm happy.

I can hear the girls playing "Paw Patrol" through the wall, and I know they have surprise birthday cupcakes waiting for me (they spilled the beans yesterday:) I've been spending an awful lot of time reflecting lately. Much to unpack there, but suffice to say this year is going to be taken up 39 notches.

Watch out world;)
#ThisIsMeNow
#ThisIsMe
#ThisIs39
#HAPPYbirthday
#MyHappyPlace"

It was a total clue to the wider world about what I was about to do: quit a career to venture out on my own self-designed path.

This was one of my most vulnerable posts. I didn't have to wait long for the reactions. The sheer positivity that poured in astounded me. I didn't get one negative comment. Not one. Maybe the authenticity just resonated with people. But men and women, older and younger, sent me nothing but simple positive energy.

This was also about the time I started to take back control of my own appearance. For eight long years, my job dictated how to present myself to the world, whether I liked it or not. Despite my desire to keep my hair long, I was instructed to keep it at my shoulders for TV. I didn't choose the colors, styles or sleeve length I wore. I didn't choose my own jewelry or lipstick colors. Meanwhile, the cost of everything—every haircut, makeup palette and article of on-air clothing— came out of my own pocket. I didn't care one bit for this arrangement.

In my last year on the air, though, I began to grow out my hair. I was growing as a person, too. My mindset became more aspirational. My attitude became more resolute. My plan for my own future started to categorically fall in line. And I no longer wanted to be controlled down to the length of my hair.

That 39th birthday post taught me a lot. It was totally liberating.

We've all got to get past the misguided notion that anyone else has any say in who we are. That includes your appearance and it includes what you stand for.

Over time, I've had countless interactions and conversations with people where I purposely amended my words to reflect what I thought they wanted to hear. I softened my opinion. I wouldn't say what I really thought.

Even as I planned my departure from TV news— the whole basis of this book—I still caught myself trying to appease. Once I was on the phone with my agent discussing this huge move, this major life decision that I was 100% set on.

"Is there any scenario where you'd consider renewing your contract with your current TV station?" he asked me.

I still blurted out, "Well, I mean it'd take a lot. They'd have to give me a better schedule. I can't work overnight anymore, and—"

Then I caught myself mid-sentence. What was I saying? I was done negotiating. Why was I still trying to say something that would compromise my desires just to appease the other side?

I knew I didn't want to continue that life.

I wasn't going back to that life.

Yet, old habits die so hard, don't they?

You are totally, 100% unique, and deserve to present yourself as you are. That's a hard thing when insecurity, outside influence and naysayers impress upon us.

Show yourself. Be yourself.

Say what you mean. Know what you stand for. And stick to it.

10

FEARLESSLY BETTER YOURSELF

> The most important relationship is the one you have with yourself."
>
> — Diane von Furstenberg

> Live as if you were to die tomorrow. Learn as if you were to live forever."
>
> — Mahatma Gandhi

A wood sign bearing 12 lines of stenciled text hangs in my stairwell.

The sign reads: "Like yourself. Dance often. Smile. Have an opinion. Dream big dreams. Believe. Read everything you can. Leave footprints. Love life. Have a plan. Persevere. Learn new things. Cry. Make a child laugh. Be the friend you'd like to have. Be daring. Live every moment. Make a difference."

I love this sign for so many reasons, for its obviously inspiring messages and the lessons I want to teach my daughters. But there's a more subtle reason I adore this wall art.

This is my first-ever attempt at woodworking and stenciling, long before I launched my DIY YouTube channel. I made this sign from wood pallet planks that I sanded smooth and stained a weathered gray. Then I hand-painted that long list of phrases I aim to live by, our version of the "rules of the house."

I got discouraged when I couldn't sand the weird discoloration off the pallet. I remember my early frustrations of working with wood glue and getting the clamps to hold the wood together just right. It was hard to line up the stenciling so it'd be straight and level all the way across. It took me weeks to complete this project. Today, though, it might take me three hours total to complete this same project, simply because I've learned and mastered the techniques.

Sure, the finished product's far from perfect. I'd prefer the edges were smoother and more even. The paint bled through my stenciling in lots of spots. I would have used a much lighter weight wood had I known better. But I learned from those mistakes and proudly hang that reminder on my wall.

No one's an instant expert.

We all start somewhere. That's how we get better.

NEVER STOP LEARNING

I've always believed that learning should never stop, whether it's gobbling up a great book, logging into a free webinar, asking Google a question or consuming a killer podcast.

The alternative is dispiriting, and I realized this the hard way. For a long stretch of several years, I abandoned learning. I just stopped absorbing. I stopped reading. I stopped watching. I stopped seeking. I stopped listening.

I just came to a halt.

Initially, I stopped seeking out new things to soak in, new skills to learn or new hobbies to try, simply from sheer exhaustion from my TV schedule. Fatigue is the ultimate energy suck. But when you throw frustrations and negativity into that mix, you find yourself in a rut. Boy, did that rut hold its grip on me.

I didn't want to do anything. When we started a family, learning anything new became even more unattainable. Raising twins on top of total tiredness created a double-whammy kibosh on any desire I might have had to pick up anything new.

Up until that point, I had always worked on learning something. There's the obvious first 20-plus years of my life that I spent in school. I earned a bachelor of arts degree, a bachelor of science, multiple certifications in fitness instruction, and lifeguard, first aid and CPR certifications, just to name a few.

An avid reader since childhood, I always loved coming across a word I didn't recognize. I'd promptly look it up on Google or, in the old days, head to the dictionary. When I became pregnant, I hoofed it straight to the parenting section of Barnes & Noble and bought a stack of books to understand and prepare for my next nine months. Shortly thereafter, I realized I needed to order more from the scant offering of books on twin parenting. I marked up those books like a fiend.

When I first moved out on my own and furnished my first place, I read books and leafed through magazines on the basics of budget decorating and interior design. For a while, documentaries on British royal history, the Roosevelts and the Civil War were my jam until I exhausted Netflix's inventory on the subjects. As Steve and I began to host our big family for holidays several times per year, I learned how to effectively plan a big party, while remaining organized, on schedule and sane all at once.

I relished the rare opportunity to tag along on my husband's business trips because I could explore new cities solo. The few chances I've had to do this have been some of the most fulfilling days I can remember. While poor Steve sat cooped up in general sessions, meetings and breakout workshops in windowless conference rooms, I gobbled up local culture. I spent an entire day walking around Miami, getting in my steps on South Beach and learning about Art Deco architecture on a self-guided walking tour. Later I strolled the stunning grounds at the Vizcaya Museum and Gardens.

New Orleans romanced me one dreary, misty day as I learned the fascinating history of voodoo and Marie Laveau's real story. I loved dining solo at Muriel's Jackson Square while reading a murder mystery novel by a famed NOLA author I had just picked up at a nearby used book store. Of course, I got a beignet and coffee afterward.

Wearing my cutoff jean shorts and cowboy boots, I felt an exhilarating wind in my hair as I explored Nashville on an electric Bird scooter. I ate southern comfort food at the historic Woolworth's lunch counter where segregation protests occurred in the 1960s. I psyched out my paranoia as I hunted for ghosts on a walking tour of the city's most haunted spots.

Those days in new cities filled my symbolic cup to the brim.

Having something new to engage and interest ourselves is energizing. When I'm excited about a new online course, a new workout, a new book or a new series of video tutorials, my motivation literally kicks me out of bed in the morning.

Here's one of my truths: Learning is my personal pilot light. It's this internal, perpetual flame of passion and interest. Feeding that hunger for new information keeps me satisfied as a human, and drives me to do more—and be more.

Losing this key part of my well-being for a few years depleted me. Extinguishing my natural curiosity on top of the mental and physical anguish I already suffered created a horrible snowball effect.

All these bad things—disinterest, irritation, anger, sadness, weight gain, poor diet, general apathy and loss of energy—fed each other.

Thankfully, I woke up.

I did my self-auditing. I did my gut checks. I began the mental and active shifting I've described to build a better existence for myself. I broke the pattern of inactivity.

I had finally figured out what I wanted to do, the pursuits that would help me check off my four keys to happiness: become an author, develop a presence as a public speaker, and create an online course, leveraging YouTube and my established online presence.

However, once I had that pinned down, I had a ton of new learning to do.

KEEP YOUR PILOT LIGHT *LIT*

Granted, I entered my new venture with a serious advantage of professional broadcasting and producing experience. That set me up to teach others the basics of video production and gave me an edge on creating my own content. But the rest of it? Psssh. I was Cher Horowitz—"Clueless."

I had no idea where to begin to write a book, who'd publish it, how I'd format it, how to design a cover or where I'd find an editor.

I had no idea how to plant a flag in the public speaking space, the most effective way to deliver a talk, how to find and book gigs, what to charge, and what to include in a keynote speech.

I had no idea how to create an online course, what tools I'd need, how to build an email marketing funnel, how to price my course and which hosting platform made the most sense for me.

Since all of these pursuits were new to me, I knew I had a lot to learn. As I drove to the station when I still worked those very early mornings, I listened to YouTube videos about video optimization and harnessing analytics. I listened to podcasts about launch teams and personal brand development on my lunchtime drive home.

On the days when I was on the road for longer than 30 minutes, I set up video playlists from YouTube channels of experts in online video, publishing and marketing. I soaked in as much as I could about how to make it on YouTube, how to self-publish a book, how to build an email list, and how to create a lead magnet and subsequently deliver it to the right people.

I soaked up Gary Vaynerchuk's and Seth Godin's keynotes as I got dolled up for a full morning of local news. I used my off-hours in the afternoons to join free webinars from experts in my aspired spaces. I invested in online courses to teach me YouTube and business-building techniques. I put entrepreneurship, branding and marketing books on hold at the library and devoured as much of them as I could before passing out in bed, only to awaken when my limp hand dropped the book onto my face. I renewed these books several times, but ended up purchasing my own copies later so I could mark up and dog-ear the most valuable pages.

Diving headfirst into personal education lit a fire in me. I was so inspired, interested, driven, motivated and ready to do the work. I was ready to create a better reality for myself. The surge of my excitement was off the charts.

Truly, this was one of the critical keys to finding my happiest existence—reigniting my love of learning.

DO YOUR OWN VERSION OF THE WHEEL

Part of your betterment process is also pushing yourself out of your comfort zone. It's important to test your limits. If you take enough fitness classes, you'll inevitably hear an instructor tell you to push yourself because you're physically capable of so much more than you think.

This is not only true, but it extends far beyond the physical. Your mind is vast and able.

You've got more in you, I guarantee it: more capacity to learn, more capacity to master and more capacity to advance physically and mentally.

Now, you have to believe it.

When I was 28 years old, I tried P90X for the first time.

If you've never heard of it, it's a 90-day, extreme

workout routine complete with weight and strength training, crazy cardiovascular work, and stretching and flexibility sessions. It's a severe understatement to say Tony Horton, the program's trainer and host, is a bit of a ham. You really had to embrace his cheesy lines (or ignore them entirely) to stick with P90X.

"Get sexy with it!"

"I recommend foot spray."

"Don't smash your face!"

"Okra? I love okra!"

"German potato soup? If that's not P90X soup, I don't know what is!"

Horton worked the letter "X" into his vocabulary as often as possible. "X me, baby!" (Ugh, what?) He had us do jumping jacks in the shape of an X. He threw an X into half the workout titles: Kenpo X, X Stretch and Ab Ripper X. My first-ever introduction to yoga? His Yoga X routine.

Ever since Yoga X, I've fallen in love with the practice and have learned a lot about how far my own limits can stretch (pun intended). But it came with a lot of self-doubt, too. Yoga poses are hard, particularly if you don't start with much flexibility. On a scale of 1 to 10, 10 being most flexible and strong, my ability fell somewhere around a 4 when I first started practicing.

In my very first Yoga X routine attempt, there were so many poses I just couldn't pull off. Crane, warrior III and standing splits—it was a struggle just getting into a plank let alone holding it. But I believed if I practiced long enough and got stronger, I'd eventually be able to do them. This turned out to be 100% true. However, at the outset, there was one pose I dismissed entirely because I never thought I'd get it.

Ugh, the dreaded wheel. OK, mister, you're telling me you want me to twist my wrists backward into the most awkward position possible, but then also push myself up so my body's in the shape of a rainbow? And then once I'm there, lift a leg straight up into the sky?

In the video, I watched women and men demonstrate this move, but I couldn't grasp how in the name of tree pose they did it. I was brand-new to anything like this, with zero gymnastics background. How do you even begin to find the balance? Where do you get the strength? I thought, "There's no way I'm ever going to do that pose."

I got completely in my own head. Every time I pushed play on that workout, I'd bail on even attempting the elusive wheel. Then, while scrolling my Facebook feed, I saw a friend who's a fellow P90X fan post that she had done the wheel pose! There was the photographic proof: She was in a backbend, one leg pointed straight to the sky.

While my friend was stronger physically than I was at the time, seeing someone I actually knew achieve the wheel pose gave me a helpful kick in the tush. The next time I did Yoga X, I refused to allow my brain to tell me I couldn't do the pose. With my back on the mat, I twisted my wrists behind my head. I breathed and started to push upward from my hands and feet. And holy shit, the next thing I knew, I was in the wheel pose.

I chickened out on trying to lift my leg that first day, but I was proud of myself for getting that far. As I continued to practice, my mindset of self-doubt and fear turned into one of confidence and willingness to try. Then one day—I'll never forget it—I had moved my workout outside to my back deck because it was such a beautiful State College day.

I knew the Yoga X routine so well by this point, that I just needed to hook the audio to our backyard speakers. I had gotten through the vinyasa and warrior series, and now it was wheel time. The smell of spring and the warm afternoon put me in a brave and positive state of mind. As I pushed up into bridge pose, I told myself I was going for full wheel today.

Via the deck speakers, Tony cued anyone who wanted to try it: "Ok, hot shots, push up into wheel."

This was it. I cautiously lifted my heel off the ground and then my toes. And shaky though I was, I managed to get my leg in the air for a few breaths.

I was shocked. Then, elated. Then, proud. As I carefully lowered back down to the mat, I had the goofiest grin on my face as I lay there, letting what I'd just achieved sink in.

I had convinced myself that I couldn't do it.

And I was dead wrong.

CURATE YOUR HAPPY RETREATS

For me, lifelong learning is the epitome of self-care. However, bettering yourself isn't just about learning and fueling your brain. Let's talk about some other key facets of self-care.

Self-care is an umbrella term for a vast cornucopia of personal nourishment. I used to associate self-care exclusively with little luxuries like manicures, pedicures and massages. Yes, pampering falls into the bucket of self-care, but it's so much more than that.

It's physical, so yes, that means aesthetics. It's your personal beauty fix: getting your hair styled and colored, doing your at-home facials and grooming, painting your toes a fun color for beach season, or applying makeup and body bronzer. It's also your diet, as you fuel and feed your body the right nutrition that will serve and energize you. It's also indulging in a decadent dessert when you want it. It's working on your physical strength, cardiovascular health and overall flexibility. It's practicing the healing effects of stretching and breathwork.

Self-care is also showing up for yourself, so you can move through this world and interact with others in a meaningful, effective and purposeful way. It's setting boundaries for yourself, learning how and when to say yes, and more importantly, when to say no (without guilt). It's professional and career development: attending conferences, taking classes and networking. It's working on relationships: keeping family close, maintaining friendships and building business contacts. Sometimes, it's knowing how and when to let certain relationships fade away for your own good.

It's devoting time and resources to develop and grow even more into all the roles you fill: spouse, parent, partner, friend, business owner or professional, and your own person. That's why I purposely seek out and consume content from kickass women: entrepreneurs, motivational speakers, authors, celebrities and fitness experts. This keeps my drive in high gear to keep working hard.

Self-care is also mental. It's practicing meditation to center yourself. It's embracing and seeking out the quiet. It's purposeful relaxation. It's practicing gratitude. It's journaling your hopes and dreams, and then brainstorming how you can turn those dreams into goals with action items to achieve them. It's finding your personal Tony Robbins-style power and confidence. It's getting in your best mindset. It's reading and listening to inspiring literature and music. It's understanding and acknowledging when you need a break from the ruckus at home or at work. It's giving yourself permission to take a walk, a bike ride or a drive to clear your head.

When I need a mood shift, I watch a video clip of my then 3-year-old daughters dancing their first-ever ballet performance as Polichinelles in "The Nutcracker Ballet." It's one of the most joyous things ever.

As the lilting strings of Tschaikovsky's "Mother Ginger and Her Polichinelles" fills the crowded-to-capacity middle school auditorium, my girls, decked out in lime green and hot pink clown costumes and headpieces, stand stock still for a few seconds. Their teachers placed them dead center purposely, knowing that being enveloped in the theatrical atmosphere might help them come out of their shells.

Suddenly, the seemingly impossible happened. Kaeden, the most pensive child I've ever met, begins to dance with a broad smile on her face like she's having the time of her life. She claps to the rhythm and then begins to do the skip-in-place step. Meanwhile, Parker's unsure. She's caught off guard by the lights, by the semi-visible sea of faces in the crowd. She continues to simply stand there.

But then, Kaeden notices that Parker isn't dancing and very dramatically taps her sister on the shoulder, as if to say, "Hey! What are you doing? Let's go, sis! It's showtime!"

Parker begins to move, clapping, toe-tapping and spinning with her arms extended over her head.

I was so proud. Tears of laughter and pride welled as I watched these two little princesses do their thing. Months later, parents still commented on their entertaining performance.

Now, this clip sits on my laptop desktop so it's readily accessible. I can quickly grab a pick-me-up that plasters an ear-to-ear grin on my face and lifts my spirits.

Here's another example: I rearranged our bedroom so I could wake to a view of the sunrise each morning. Simple, yes. Motivating? You're damn right. Make tiny adjustments as you need them, feng shui or otherwise, to curate these tiny happy retreats for yourself.

That's the definition of self-care.

DUMP THE GUILT GROUP, STAT

I'm not saying you need to schedule a weekly manicure, meet up with a different friend every Friday, travel to every conference in your industry, meditate every morning, journal every night, develop a six-days per week exercise regimen and host family dinners at your place every Sunday.

However, from a list of self-care items, you should pick a few that you know can serve you. Listen to yourself honestly. If your instinct tells you that changing your dietary habits is a smart, healthy idea, your gut is giving you clues that you should try it. If your heartfelt reaction to the idea of purposeful, devoted relaxation practice is, "I wish I had time for that," listen to yourself and give it a go. If you read a description of an online continuing education class and think, "I'd love to try that," trust yourself, and at least do some research on it.

We can find an excuse not to do literally anything. Resist that temptation. Take the baby steps you need to try something new. If it feels right, slowly develop a habit from there. If your life is lacking in physical, mental or developmental self-care, it's vital to your well-being to address these voids. You deserve to carve out time for yourself to develop rituals, habits and practices that fuel and feed your soul.

Self-care is like in-flight rules. In case of a loss of pressure during a flight, we know oxygen masks will drop from above our seats. The rule is to put your own mask on first before you help anyone else with theirs. It's the ultimate analogy for self-care. You'll be no help to anyone if you lose consciousness trying to care for everyone else, before you secure your own safety and well-being.

Your heart might be in the right place as you put everyone else first. I applaud your heroism and desire to care for others above yourself. But let's face it: If you've passed out in your airplane seat, you've created a bigger problem for yourself and those around you. Likewise, you can't be the best version of yourself as a person, spouse, parent, boss, co-worker or friend if you're not taking care of yourself. This was another lesson learned the hard way, because I didn't take care of myself for the longest time. I saddled myself with a membership to what I called The Guilt Group for way too long.

Meet The Guilt Group. That's the group of women, particularly mothers, who can't bring themselves to do things strictly for themselves because it feels selfish and they're overwrought with unshakeable guilt at the mere thought of it. We Guilt Groupers don't think we should leave our babies to grab lunch with a girlfriend. We can't rationalize getting a sitter so we might indulge in a professional pedicure and the luxury of an uninterrupted hour. We Guilt Groupers feel overwhelming distress at the thought of dumping our kids on our spouses or partners to take a quiet afternoon to ourselves to sit on a park bench with a book or go shopping alone.

When I went back to work after having twins, I religiously rushed home after work every day to jump in and help care for our daughters. My husband was handling a huge load by himself for the first half of the day. He woke with the girls every weekday and kept them occupied, fed, changed and out of trouble until I got home—all while busting his tail like a superman for his work-from-home job (and he got promoted twice while doing all of this).

Since I knew Steve was working hard to balance work and home by himself, I felt like I owed it to him to rush home as quickly as possible to help out. That meant I struggled to get in any measure of self-care, which in hindsight, I desperately needed. Guess what? He never gave me grief for taking time for myself when I needed it.

This whole guilt complex was completely in my head, as you've probably realized.

It was up to me to settle it for myself.

GET HEALTHY, ONCE AND FOR ALL

After my girls were born, I developed an extreme case of "mommy brain".

I'd go to retrieve some object from the bedroom, and forget what I went to grab by the time I climbed the stairs. I'd space on what day we expected a storm system while live on the air. I had trouble conjuring certain words in the middle of conversations. My brain didn't seem to want to function properly, to the point I became concerned for my health.

I sought the advice from a doctor friend (who made regular appearances on the morning show). He stressed firmly that this was more than typical new parent fatigue, and that I *must* get more sleep.

I remained stuck in a vicious, exhausted cycle, however. Working my bizarre TV schedule for so long nulled out all the self-care basics for me: adequate sleep, adequate exercise and a good diet. Up until September 18, 2019, when I experienced my first weekday with no 2:45 a.m. alarm, these fundamental practices weren't attainable for me.

The rigor of the overnight schedule automatically meant I didn't have a prayer of getting enough sleep. I didn't have the energy to devote to even 30 minutes of regular, daily exercise. And what I ate? Well, we ate takeout far too often. In fairness, I was more disciplined at work. I packed a very well-rounded lunch of healthy and filling foods like packaged salmon, a LÄRABAR, Greek yogurt and a hard-boiled egg. I almost never indulged in the ice cream, doughnuts, candy, cookies, muffins, bagels and pizza that always showed up in the newsroom.

Unfortunately, by the time I'd get home, my constant exhaustion meant I always lost my will to avoid the foods I knew would make my body feel terrible after I ate them. That's why I was 10 pounds overweight for a long time. While that's not huge in the grand scheme, I wanted to be healthier. I wanted to feel stronger. I wanted to fit into my clothes better. On top of it all, I was always on camera, which enhances flaws you don't see in the mirror.

I've always had a pooch. You know, that little extra bulge of fat right below your belly button. I could never exercise it away. And of course, it showed on TV. People routinely asked me on social media if I was expecting again. If you Googled my name, "Is Katie Fehlinger pregnant again?" showed up in the autofill results. Ugh, it was so embarrassing. My solution? I sucked in my gut as best I could, wore flare skirts as often as possible, and layered on the shapewear underneath.

However, setting the concrete date to call it a career in morning TV turned out to be a catalyst for change on the fitness front. By this point, I had spent four years pouring my heart, soul, life and my everything into caring for my girls. But how could I be the best version of myself as a mother or spouse if I didn't take the steps to feel my best?

I needed to start taking care of me, too.

From the first day after I stopped setting my 2:45 a.m. alarm, I exercised at least six days a week. I voraciously worked on developing a smarter diet. I made time for myself by just sitting on the swing chair in our backyard with a book.

But most importantly in all this, I got out of my head.

I chucked my Guilt Group membership. No one (save for a few internet trolls) shamed me for not spending enough time with my children.

Gradually, I worked my guilt-laden mindset into one of self-love.

Today, my mindset is healthier and happier than it's ever been.

I'm physically fitter and stronger than ever, even as I'm pushing 40. In fact, I didn't feel this good in my 20s.

The joy I've discovered from just allowing myself to cultivate my life, my physical and mental health, my relationships, and my professional development is priceless.

We all deserve that.

Nurture those corners of your being that need your attention to flourish.

Be kind to your body and soul.

Take care of you.

11
HAVE A GOOD SHOW

> Cry in the beginning, so you can smile in the end."
>
> — Marta Vieira da Silva

> I'd rather have a lifetime of 'Oh, wells' than 'What ifs'."
>
> — Unknown

At 11:56 a.m. on a Tuesday, I was miked up, clicker in hand, ifb in my ear, waiting for our noon show, "Talk Philly," to start.

Suddenly, I heard my producer, Monica, intone pleasantly, "Have a good show!"

Monica is one of the best producers out there. Her pre-show routine always includes a quick second to connect with the anchors from the control room by wishing us a good show. I got so used to hearing those words, but they always gave me a lift. I stood a little straighter, displayed more confidence and mustered up a tad more pizzazz as the show began.

"Have a good show" could have meant, "Hope your graphics system doesn't crash" or "Good luck spitting out three minutes of ad-libbed weather information on the fly while sounding coherent" or "Knock 'em dead by not tripping over the cables on the studio floor."

These days, I prefer to think of those words as having a dramatically bigger message.

Have a good show.

Look at the biggest possible picture in that short little sentence.

Life is our show.

Our existence on this planet and the time we spend on it is our show. Our experiences, goals, work and relationships should all be the show.

Each day is our show.

Every decision is our show.

I don't know about you, but I want to have a damn good show.

The key to having a great show is waking up each day with a purpose. I've finally figured that out for myself, and I hope that throughout this book you've latched onto some nuggets of my story that you relate to, or want to work toward for yourself.

Whether you need time, motivation or discipline to figure out what your "good show" looks like, do yourself a solid and just start.

Time will pass regardless. You might as well use it.

As you work toward actualizing your "good show," you'll need tactics to help you sustain what you've worked so hard to accomplish. I want to share some strategies that made a world of difference for me since my crazy life-shifting journey began.

BE PATIENT

When I started my DIY YouTube channel, my subscriber growth moved at a snail's pace.

I knew not to expect too much, but I had high hopes for some decent upward movement out of the gate. Despite having more than 28,000 followers on Facebook, 17,000 on Twitter and 4,000 on Instagram at the time, I didn't make much headway those first few months.

Thankfully, a number of people subscribed right away simply because they wanted to support my side project. However, it took me almost four months to build up to 500 subscribers, even with an already-established following on other platforms.

I refused to get discouraged. Rather, I sent out a big "thank you" to those amazing 500 people who showed me support right at the beginning. My number of followers could only go up from there—and it did, to more than 19,000 as I write this.

I viewed this as an eye-on-the-prize situation. As I hustled to solo-produce and film each of my 50 (and climbing) DIY videos, I realized I was building something bigger than a follower count.

DIY Lesson Learned: Keep at it. Big goals take big time. Invest in yours and wait for it.

DO THE WORK

Nothing just gets handed to you.

Any big project, just like any big success, requires you dig in the trenches for a while, likely a long while, without any or much of any return on the work you're putting in. Whether your goal is to lose that last 15 pounds of baby weight, write a book, start your own business, redesign your backyard or just organize your really messy attic, you need to appreciate your time commitment. All of it takes time. You must actively work toward that end goal in mini steps that progressively get you to the finish line.

Rachel Hollis echoes this idea in her book, "Girl, Stop Apologizing." You can't overwhelm yourself by saying you're going to complete one huge project. Break it down into manageable tasks you can realistically complete.

Each night before bed, I make a list of exactly what I want to accomplish the next day in a note on my phone called "Tomorrow." Your list of action items can be as detailed as you want. I like to get specific. Rather than just devoting a set amount of hours to various projects, I write out very precisely what I want to check off with a digestible set of tasks, like this:

TOMORROW

- Write social copy for this week's video.
- Follow up with Dan.
- Research keywords for cross-stitch tutorial series.
- Write 500 words.
- Create 4 video thumbnails.

- 60-minute yoga workout.
- Load of the girls' laundry.

I can check off all of these in one day. That allows me to tackle stuff without overwhelming myself, and it gives me a confidence boost since I achieve what I set out to do. I get the warmest fuzzy of satisfaction when I can cross a completed item off my daily list. Breaking down big projects into sets of subtasks helps you get the work done more effectively.

Another one of my strategies for success? Don't talk about the work. Just do it. Try doing the work quietly without fanfare and letting your success be the noise. In other words, don't shout from the rooftops what you're going to do. Shout from the rooftops what you've already done.

That said, accountability is a good thing. If you're a procrastinator working to finish the first draft of a book or if you're trying to lose weight, it may serve you to have some cheerleaders behind you. Join a Facebook or LinkedIn group of like-minded people. Attend local meetups, clubs or business functions to find a support group of people doing the exact same thing you are. You might even find a mentor who's ahead of you on your path, and can offer some great insights.

DIY Lesson Learned: Start each day with a plan of attack. You'll be so much more productive. And remember, don't spend so much of your time telling everyone what you're about to do.

Just do it.

GET ORGANIZED

A lot of people have asked me since I gave birth to twins, "How do you do it all?" Well, I've got some not-so-secret weapons.

For starters, I have a true partner in my husband. I couldn't keep my head screwed on straight if it weren't for his willingness to help, his near-constant good nature and his friendship. Besides the assistance from fellow humans, I have one main weapon in my sanity arsenal: organization.

Martha Stewart once said, "Life is too complicated not to be orderly." Staying organized keeps me content. I'm not exaggerating when I say keeping my constant swirl of mental reminders, tasks, appointments, events and planning lists all neatly organized is absolutely critical for me to not only get shit done, but also to be happy.

I personally stay organized with lots of lists. Along with my daily task list, I also keep a running "Things to Accomplish" note on my phone. This list is a working document of groceries we're running out of, random errands I need to run and projects I want to try. I've always jotted things down the second I think of them because they'd flit out of my brain the next second otherwise. For example, when the clock struck 4:03 a.m. and I was deep in makeup application and realized my liquid eyeliner was drying out, I'd whip out my Notes app and immediately jot it in there.

I also look ahead months vs. days or weeks in my calendar.

When my daughters turned 2 years old, we threw a pretty epic DIY Sesame Street-themed birthday party. I went all out creating homemade games, decor and fun food. Oscar the Grouch's Garbage Toss. A DIY streetlight made from a styrofoam ball, bright green spray-painted shipping tubes and a planter pot. Chocolate and rainbow sprinkle-covered pretzel wands that paid homage to Abby Cadabby. Fruit and veggie trays artfully arranged to portray the likenesses of Elmo, Oscar and Big Bird.

In order to finish all of the party elements within an inch of my sanity, I started planning three months in advance. I slowly knocked out what could be done eight weeks prior: character-themed menu cards, the Hooper's Store sign that would hang above the garage and the "This Party Is Brought to You by the Letters P and K" chalkboard sign that welcomed our guests up the driveway.

DIY Lesson Learned: When you methodically lay out

a plan and keep meticulous notes and lists, you'll keep yourself focused and on track, ensuring you get everything done.

BE PRACTICAL

Leaving a job by choice when you have mouths to feed, along with a mortgage and car payments, is no joke. Look, I have the most encouraging spouse on the planet. But no matter how much I wanted this change or how much support Steve gave me, the bills still came. I had roughly 14 months left on my TV contract when I started seriously considering my departure.

We spent that time scaling back on expenses, saving as much as possible and rearranging our accounts in the smartest way possible. We did a lot of math, figuring out how we could break even if we lost an entire salary, making conscious choices about how we approached money to make sure this would work once my regular income was gone. I was completely willing to take a pay cut. But I couldn't make peace with that choice if it meant putting unreasonable stress on our finances. How was I going to fulfill this vital shift in my life and still maintain what we had worked so hard for? How would we pay the mortgage? How would we be comfortable without me having a guaranteed income?

I'm all about being deservedly selfish with your own

happiness and going after something you want. But, you also have to assess real life. Even after I settled on leaving my TV career and starting on a new solopreneur path from scratch, I still needed to wait and work toward it. I paid off credit cards while I still had an income. I busted my tail with any free time I had to work ahead on my YouTube channel. I learned email marketing and affiliate marketing, and so many other key skills I'd need to pull off the ambitious ventures I wanted to pursue. I wrote as much of this book as I could in any spare time I could find, and outlined the lessons and modules for my online course.

I took my time and planned for this huge move, and firmly believed I needed to consider other people. I have two children and their future to consider. I have a husband who has done me the biggest solid any human can do for another, by having my back unconditionally through every stage of my life since we met. He's the one who'd shoulder the financial burden if I don't succeed. I couldn't disregard Steve's role in all this, since my move would directly affect and impact him and our children.

As the months progressed, things started lining up in our situation as if some higher power was giving me every reason to make the change. I knew we'd be OK. But to get there, I planned. A lot.

If you have a dream you want to pursue, employ

practicality so you can have a solid, reasonable roadmap to make it happen. Reverse-engineer it: How much money do you need to earn to maintain your current lifestyle, or at least stay afloat? Where are you with that goal right now? You may need to side hustle, while maintaining a full-time job, unless you're willing to give up some big things. I wasn't in that place. Steve and I agreed we weren't about to uproot our 3-year-olds from the only home they've ever known and all that we'd worked to provide for them.

Think long and hard about what your dream life is worth to you. Are you willing to give up your house or apartment and move back in with parents or crash on a friend's couch until you can get on your feet? Are you willing to give up Grubhub orders or the organic produce you love? Are you willing to bag the vacation you wanted to take this summer? How does your 401(k) look? Do you have a nest egg? Are you OK with dipping into your savings if you had to?

Map out the path that makes sense for you. It didn't make sense for me to bail on my paycheck unless we could initially get by each month on Steve's income and the money I knew I could make in the first few months after leaving my salaried job.

DIY Lesson Learned: Along your road to happiness, tough choices come into play, but you can and should plan for them as best you can.

Answer these questions to get your wheels turning: What are the risks you face if you uproot? What will your living situation look like? How will you pay bills? Do you have a support system financially? Emotionally?

CONTINUE YOUR GUT CHECKS

On a lazy, cold January Sunday afternoon, Steve and I sat on the couch, each with our iPhones in hand as Pro Bowl pregame coverage droned in the background. I was playing an addicting Candy Crush-type game as he scrolled his Twitter feed, both of us keeping one eye and ear aimed outside where the girls were bundled and playing with their balance bikes and sidewalk chalk.

Our family had just returned from a winter weekend refresh at the beach. The sun was out, and it was windy and cold, one of those days that begs you to just veg on the couch, snuggle under a blanket and do a whole lot of nothing.

And then.

"What?" Steve said to his phone in disbelief.

"What?" I asked him.

A pause.

"TMZ is reporting that Kobe Bryant died in a helicopter crash," he said.

Neither of us spoke for a while. Steve kept scrolling,

looking and waiting for updates. I opened Twitter and read through all my former news colleagues' feeds, seeing what insider tips they may have gotten about this horrific rumor and any indication as to whether it was actually true.

We all know how much worse a story this became.

The day was hard to process. Big events went on as scheduled around the country, but with a dark shadow cast over them.

We watched as Pro Bowlers paid respect with touchdown tributes and listened as the announcers tried to hold their emotions together. That night, I shed a lot of tears as we watched the Grammys. My lip quivered as Alicia Keys and Boyz II Men sang "It's So Hard to Say Goodbye" a cappella. I couldn't stop the tears streaming down my face as Camila Cabello performed a moving, beautiful tribute to her father, made even more poignant given what had happened hours earlier.

My head, mind and soul ached for the Bryants' loss of a father and husband, and a daughter and sister. I couldn't begin to think how a tragedy so unspeakable would affect me. This hit me in my gut. It was so terrible and relatable. My own husband was barely three months younger than Kobe when his helicopter went down. Steve too is a #girldad, a hashtag that began trending after ESPN's Elle Duncan tearfully recounted a conversation she had with Kobe where he'd expressed how much he loved being a dad to girls.

This tragedy was a gut check, a reminder I didn't know I needed to hug my girls and husband tighter.

A FEW WEEKS LATER, I felt groggy. Our increasingly annoying, grumpy old cat, Pumpkin, had woken me up too early, his stinky, in-my-face meows letting me know he wanted breakfast. I sat in an armchair drinking coffee, trying to summon the energy to get my day moving. I mindlessly played another dumb game on my phone as Parker kept asking me questions.

"Mommy, what pants are you going to wear tomorrow when you drop us off in the car line?"

"Mommy, are your pants blue or green?"

"Mommy, what shoes do you like?"

"Mommy, will you wear your black shoes or your brown shoes when you take us to school?"

I was out of it, still half-asleep, and starting to get irritated with the incessant and seemingly pointless questions. I know I got short with her. She finally left me alone for a few minutes. But eventually, she returned to my side and leaned over my armchair.

"Mommy, I made you a picture."

I looked up from my phone and set it down. As she

handed me her drawing, she excitedly revealed, "It's a picture of you!"

Indeed it was. There in colorful marker was a stick figure dressed in blue pants and brown shoes. In this portrait, my potato-shaped, bald head was tilted to one side and I had outstretched stick arms with three fingers on each hand, as if I was ready to give a big hug. Two large emerald-colored circles dotted the inside of my head.

"I made your eyes green because your eyes are green!"

Gut check.

All of Parker's prattling questions made sense now. She just wanted to get the details right for the drawing she was making just for me. Holding back tears, I stretched my arms open wide just like the portrait my sweet girl gave me and wrapped her in a huge hug. We sat there for a while in a snuggle, until she said she wanted to hang the picture on the window by my bed. With that, she bolted to the kitchen to find some tape.

Ferris Bueller wisely put it, "Life moves pretty fast. If you don't stop and look around once in a while, you could miss it."

DIY Lesson Learned: Let in those reminders and gut checks. Hug your loved ones tightly and tell them you love them. Every. Single. Day.

DON'T QUIT YOUR DAYDREAM

I have a girl crush on Sara Blakely, the founder and CEO of Spanx. If you remember, she sent me a care package of baby gear and Spanx products when she heard that I got body-shamed on social media while pregnant. That gesture alone told me everything I ever need to know about her.

But aside from her fundamentally kind nature, this woman is an inspiration to me on so many additional levels. She's a strong mother, exceptionally successful entrepreneur and generous philanthropist. She's strategic and smart. She's courageous. And she lets nothing hold her back. I've followed her on social media for a few years now. While her posts are always entertaining or inspirational, one in particular caught my eye a while back. It was a picture of her holding a coffee mug that read, "Don't Quit Your Daydream."

This post was part of a full-blown campaign called #MondayMugShot. Every Monday, as many of us started the weekly grind, Ms. Blakely posted a selfie holding up a coffee mug printed with a motivational message to support other women.

Inspiration, indeed. She showed off an array of mugs all with different messages: "Girls Just Wanna Be CEO," "Good Things Come to Those Who Hustle," "You Did Not Wake Up Today to Be Mediocre" and

"Yeah, I Run Like a Girl. Try to Keep Up." Other mug-messages were just plain entertaining. "Be the CEO Your Parents Always Wanted You to Marry" made me laugh out loud. "Running Late Is My Cardio" isn't far off for me. And "More Issues Than Vogue"? Please. Any hustling mama needs a subscription, she's got so many.

I love this idea so much. I'm all about plastering phrases that elicit a smile or a bit of confidence on everyday objects. Put cute sayings on my knick-knacks, wall art, T-shirts and pouches? Yes to all of it, please.

I have a screen printed cosmetic pouch that serves as a reminder to "Keep Your Lashes Long and Your Standards High." I have a muscle tank that won't let me forget with hard work there are "No Days Off." I have a framed piece of wall art hanging in the dining room that makes sure "Today I Choose Joy."

While I have nowhere the mug collection Ms. Blakely does, one of my favorites bears the phrase, "Be Your Own Boss #BYOBoss." I purposely save it for the days I need to be even more productive. Drinking my signature hazelnut dark roast from that specific mug gives me more energy, I swear.

"Don't Quit Your Daydream." There was something about that message that resonated with me more than the rest, mostly because I came across it at a time that I really needed it. It's a perfect twist on "Don't Quit Your Day Job," the very decision I'd been wrestling with for months. Should I leave the career I'd established over so many years? But more than that, those four little words embodied something I desperately wanted for myself. My daydream was to take ownership of my life, to turn it into an existence I was excited to wake up to every morning. To work on professionally challenging, rewarding projects. To foster my relationships with my girls, my husband and all the other people who matter to me in this life.

In short, I had a daydream of just being totally happy. The idea of that becoming reality was so sweet, but it required that I take a leap I was terrified to take at the time. To make the dream reality, I had no choice. Somewhere in her timeline, Ms. Blakely included another #MondayMugShot: "Be Scared and Do It Anyway."

If you want something bad enough, you can't stop working for it because you're afraid. You have to push through the fear. You have to accept you'll make mistakes, and proceed with imperfection. It's that plain and simple. It's just not that easy, so you'll need resolve, gumption, initiative and will.

DIY Lesson Learned: Please don't settle. Whatever your daydream is, don't quit it. And find and post the messages that will keep you strong and determined to hit your goal everywhere you need to see them.

ASSESS YOUR VITALS

Part of this book was written from the driver's seat of my car.

I neared the finish of the first draft when confirmed cases of COVID-19 began to skyrocket in the U.S. We all had to transition into a new way of working and living. Because I'm the type who desperately needs zero distractions to focus, I had to get creative to meet the deadline I'd set for myself.

Since dine-in establishments had closed temporarily, I could no longer work in my preferred coffee shop setting.

I couldn't find the quiet at home since school had been cancelled indefinitely and the kids were stuck in the house.

I couldn't comfortably sit outside because the pandemic hit during the still-chilly transition from winter to spring.

Instead, I took mini road trips to peaceful empty drive-up spots with picturesque views. A shopping center paved lot, elementary school visitor space and a recreation center parking area all served as my portable office locations. I set up my cramped digs to be as comfy and conducive to productivity as possible, armed with fully charged devices, a cozy blanket and an unlit candle to place on the dashboard. Spare gloves and a mask sat in the console should I need to stop off anywhere to fill up the gas tank or hit up one of the few open Starbucks drive-thrus for a peppermint mocha (which felt like a luxury by that point).

Finishing a book is an undertaking anyway. The added weight of dealing with this new norm sent me through a range of emotions, making focus difficult. My mindset never stayed consistent. I felt stress, gratitude, anger, joy, stir craziness, calmness, fear, resolve, helplessness or optimism depending on the day.

I'd go from feeling sweet delight at spending an afternoon picnicking and playing with my girls in the backyard one day to overwhelm at having to homeschool two preschoolers. Just settling them in front of the computer for their group circle time on Zoom came with serious tension.

COVID-19 affected the entire world. Each of us has a story about its impact on us personally. Mine became one of reflection.

Life during a stay-at-home order forced a slower pace, and brought me to realize things both simple and complex:

How much I missed going to the library.

How long I can go without a haircut before I become a real life Rapunzel.

How critical my actions are to the health of those in my community.

How often I touch my face.

How heroic our health care workers really are.

Just how good a hug feels.

What I take for granted.

What I can do without.

What's truly necessary.

This strange time solidified my decision to DIY my own happiness. COVID-19 proved that life will still get complicated, distracting and frustrating. Like everyone else, nearly all my personal and business events got cancelled or put on hold. During the months-long quarantine, my productivity and energy swung like a pendulum. But at the end of each day, I could still say I was happy in the grand scheme. If coronavirus could upend the world and I could still—at my core—feel content in the choices I'd made, I knew I'd done exactly what I needed for myself.

DIY Lesson Learned: Taking away or limiting parts of our lives can shine a light on what's vital and most precious. Recognize what's most necessary to you.

BE YOUR OWN KIND OF GINGER SNAP

All of this advice falls under a big umbrella of ninja tricks, tools and tactics that have helped me.

Throughout these chapters, I've explained how I've come to define happiness, how I figured out what that looks like for me and how I got to my happy place. But happiness is a very personal thing. Happiness requires reflection to figure out. It's OK to take your time to decide what your personal, most joyous existence looks like. And once you do…

Do YOU.

I recently spent a girls' weekend in New York City to celebrate and toast my dear friend Jenna, who was getting married in a few months. It was two delightfully decadent days jam-packed with activities for us to let loose.

A piano bar and specialty shots, made just for the beautiful bride-to-be. A Beyoncé-style dance class that taught us a killer group routine to "Run the World (Girls)" to perform later at the nightclub. (We didn't, but only because the opportunity didn't present itself. But if you dig through my social media posts, you'll find the studio rehearsal.) Oh, and lots and lots of margaritas, guacamole and quesadillas. But the pinnacle of the party was the Saturday night drag queen show.

The 10 of us got dressed up in leather, leopard, sequins, heels and big hair to party like a squad. The venue was decked out for Christmas with every vibrant color imaginable. Christmas balls, baubles, beads and tall, skinny artificial trees in a technicolor palette created a gaudy and gorgeous environment.

We ordered our entrees and eagerly awaited the

show. After we finished our salad course, took a handful of group selfies and secured a plastic tiara for our guest of honor, the lights lowered, the music began pumping and an energetic high-pitched voice came over the speakers to introduce the opening act: three queens in coordinating draped dresses lip-syncing to the "Glee" cast version of "Survivor/I Will Survive." The show was freaking magical, with queens lip-syncing sets of Britney Spears, Pink, Cardi B, and Carrie Underwood, throwing in full splits on stage and mid-performance lap dances.

But the evening peaked when our show host, Ginger Snap, took the stage. Ginger kept the crowd pumped as she introduced each act. She brought the birthday girls (and guys) and brides on stage for some good-natured ribbing. She was a saucy spitfire and a half.

A short-statured, stocky queen, Ginger looked like the offspring of comedian Patton Oswalt and Sharon Osbourne. Dolled to the max in a silver bodysuit, a cinched black leather belt and knee-high black boots, she oozed attitude. She wore falsies on both her upper and lower lashes. Her lipstick was the hottest shade of Barbie girl pink with glitter that caught every stage light. She topped it all off with a short spiky wig in the most vibrant shade of neon purple. Just stunning.

The music started low and built slowly as Ginger took the stage. The crowd murmured and uttered an audible gasp as we realized what song she was about to perform. Nearly everyone recognized the quiet, slow tempo piano chords of the opening stanzas to "This Is Me" from "The Greatest Showman." As I listened, the gravity of the message started to hit me:

> *I've learned to be ashamed of all my scars.*
> *Run away, they say.*
> *No one'll love you as you are.*
> *But I won't let them break me down to dust.*
> *I know that there's a place for us.*
> *For we are glorious.*

Everything, everything about this performance was beautiful. This queen, comfortable in her own skin, not giving a shit what any of us or anyone in the fucking world thought about her. With gestures that were broad, intense and clearly full of raw emotion, Ginger felt this song, as did the rest of us. The lyrics continued to shake me:

> *When the sharpest words wanna cut me down,*
> *I'm gonna send a flood, gonna drown them out.*
> *This is brave, this is bruised.*
> *This is who I'm meant to be. This is me.*

Three-quarters through the song, a dramatic quiet pause took over for a two-count. And it was at this point that Ginger Snap, in her made-up, glam and bedazzled glory, stepped upstage center and faced the curtain.

And then, it was as if it happened in slow motion.

The beat, the singers and the full array of instruments all came in for the song's climactic finish. That's when Ginger whipped around to face the crowd.

And on the downbeat of the full ensemble's entrance, she reached up to her vibrant wig, gripping a fistful of neon purple hair. With a swift sweep of her strong hand, Ginger tore off the headpiece to reveal a black, closely shaved crew cut underneath.

We all lost it. People cheered. People cried. People threw money at her as she fiercely strutted off the stage and into the crowd to share the moment as she continued to lip-sync:

> *Look out 'cause here I come.*
> *And I'm marching on to the beat I drum.*
> *I'm not scared to be seen. I make no*
>   *apologies.*
> *This is me.*

This diva was the embodiment of having a "good show."

Should this tale ever make it back Ms. Ginger Snap,

I want her to know that moment was a rally cry for me. She roused my senses, with the vision of her crazy-beautiful sparkle and shine. The electricity of a totally entranced audience hanging on her every beat. And the rich enveloping sound of Keala Settle's voice over a booming sound system. And thanks to Ms. G, "This Is Me" is my new anthem when I need motivational power.

I HOPE my stories leave you with this: Gang, we all deserve to be who we're meant to be.

Whether you're a professional stuck in a great job you hate or a mother stuck in a routine, but desperate to start an entrepreneurial project, know that you can do it.

If you want it bad enough, you'll get past the roadblocks and the fear.

Persevere.

It's no cakewalk.

You'll put in a lot of hard work. It took me a solid year to logistically plan how I'd leap into this new life.

But it's not too late for change. It's never too late.

Do YOU.

Be who you're meant to be.

Be happy.

And have a good show.

ACKNOWLEDGMENTS

I have so many people to thank.

Steve, my actual rock: You're my best friend, love of my life, number one unwavering supporter and shoulder to lean on. There aren't enough words to describe what you mean to me. Father of the Year, Husband of the Decade, Friend of a Lifetime, I love you.

Parker and Kaeden, my sweet girls, my everything: Time has simultaneously flown by and stood still since the day you two were born. Being your mommy is my biggest achievement in this life. I'm so grateful I get to wake up with you every morning. You make me happier than anything.

Mom: You didn't just teach me through your words. You showed me with your actions what a resilient, independent, strong woman looks like. Thank you for your ever-constant encouragement.

Kevin and the entire Bloom Family: Thank you for trusting me with the honor of sharing Steph's empowering story.

My State College squad: You're the best around. Nothing's gonna ever keep you down. I love you guys beyond words.

The virtual community that has followed my journey: You made a terrifying choice a no brainer. Your support is humbling, and your kind words and love over the years have meant the world. Thank you.

The people that saw something in me: Dan, you've always encouraged me. Mrs. Bracy, you made middle school a blast. I owe so much of my confidence to you both.

My editor, Nicole Rollender: Thank you for your adeptness, perspective and insight.

My cover art designer, Josh Gragg: It's a comfort putting a vision in your hands.

A final shout out to the literature, music and movies that spoke to me through every stage of life: Having characters and artistic expressions I can relate to will forever be invaluable to me.

MY TOP 10 RESOURCES

I had much to learn as I reinvented myself and launched into new professional spaces. Here are the tools, books and people that helped and inspired me most:

SELF-AUDIT

"My Big 4 Keys to Happy" Workbook
 katiefehlinger.com

Year in Pixels Worksheet
 katiefehlinger.com

YOUTUBE

Sunny Lenarduzzi
 youtube.com/sunnylenarduzzi

Think Media
youtube.com/THiNKmediaTV

PUBLISHING

Self-Publishing School
self-publishingschool.com

Kindlepreneur with Dave Chesson
kindlepreneur.com

PUBLIC SPEAKING

The Successful Speaker
Grant Baldwin

ONLINE BUSINESS

Amy Porterfield
amyporterfield.com

Superfans: The Easy Way to Stand Out, Grow Your Tribe, and Build a Successful Business
Pat Flynn
(I love his videos, too!: youtube.com/patflynn)

Building a StoryBrand: Clarify Your Message So Customers Will Listen
Donald Miller

Made in the USA
Monee, IL
27 July 2020